"Abby has put her passion for nursing and her patients into *Naked Hope*. Her dedication, her sincerity, her compassion and her love of our profession come through beautifully. A fascinating, insightful, sincere, look from the inside: a must read for anyone thinking about becoming a nurse, and for those who wonder what nursing is really like. It provides a window into to the day-to-day transition of a new graduate nurse into one who demonstrates the best of our profession."

Elizabeth A. Murphy, BScN, MSBA, RN, NEA-BC, FACHE
Vice President and Chief Nursing Officer
Trinity Health - Saint Mary's Health Care

Naked Hope

Abby Jackson
with Greg Smith

Black Lake Press
TELL YOUR STORY
BLACKLAKEPRESS.COM

Black Lake Press
TELL YOUR STORY
BLACKLAKEPRESS.COM

Cover design by Rod Hunting.

Published by Black Lake Press of Holland, Michigan. Black Lake Press is a division of Black Lake Studio, LLC. Direct inquiries to Black Lake Press at www.blacklakepress.com.

ISBN 978-0-9839602-9-4

Dedicated to the best nurse I know—my Grandma.

Table of Contents

Acknowledgements

Thanks to:

To Tyler: My love. My heart. My compass. For not letting me quit. For seeing me and the story in me. For believing for me.

To my Grandma: For praying me through nursing school. For giving me the gift of the porcelain nurse.

Professor Crandall: Who failed me in nursing ethics. You taught me how beautiful failure can be.

To Dee Springer: For constantly reminding me of the bigger picture and helping me process and grow and smile and love on days when I feel totally empty. I wouldn't have stayed in this without you.

To Dawn Borreson: For calling me to be the best. For caring contagiously and teaching me what it really means to be a nurse.

To Roy Clark: For telling me I needed to write. You were right.

To Greg Smith: For patiently coaching and cracking the whip. Can't tell you how grateful I am. You deserve an award for all the hours of emotional turmoil you endured with me.

To the nurses and physicians: I am privileged to work with an incredible group of men and women who are making a difference in the world. Every day I learn from you. Thanks for contributing to so many of these stories. I would not be the nurse I am today if it wasn't for many of you. You took a messy and very green little nurse and gave me space to learn. Thank you.

In addition a far too short list of everyone to whom I owe thanks for helping (in no particular order): my Mom and Dad, Laura Cronin, Liz Murphy, Rod Hunting (cover photo guy) for an awesome cover design, Miriam and Sabrina, the staff at "my office" (aka Rowster's coffee for an endless supply of great almond mochas), my new parents; Tim and Cole Jackson, Victor Saad, Black Lake Press staff (Greg Smith, Sarah Brummels, Rob Stam, and Jami Vander Kooi), Dave VanderArk, Connie and Dee for getting excited for me, JR, the 7 North staff for getting me started, Nancy Crowe, Julie Ludwig, and Lisbeth Votruba for being incredible examples of nursing leadership, 3 Lacks staff, and Claire, Laura, Mel, Kim for reading all the early messy stuff.

Introduction

I see naked people.

Before most people get out of bed and shake cereal into their bowl, I've seen a dozen naked bodies. Hairy backs and belly buttons. Fit and flabby, firm and flaccid. Skin that's tanned, skin that's freckled, and skin with moles and little hairs growing out of them. Limbs with spider veins revealing a lifetime of bodily neglect and decades-old stretch marks that hint at stories I will never hear. I see fat: rolls and folds and jowls. Round, bouncy bellies perched on top of large limbs, protruding so far the owners haven't seen their genitals in years. Most of the bodies I see are old, but the real old ones aren't real fat— not too many fat people live into their eighties. Some are modest, folding and re-folding the flimsy paper-thin gown in an attempt to hide their own personal folds, and some are closet exhibitionists, flamboyant and free, eager for an excuse to drop their gown. But all gowns come up or off at some point, because my job is to minister to their naked state. I prod and poke and measure and palpate and auscultate and wipe and wash and catheterize them.

Bodies. I touch them everyday. Old bodies. Sick bodies. Wrinkled bodies. Sad bodies. Scared bodies. Tender bodies. Angry bodies. Lonely bodies. It's a weird job I have. To touch and to heal bodies. To listen, to intervene, to teach, and to assess bodies. To be an advocate for a body. To care for the body, mind, spirit ... of a stranger; all for strangers. Strangers in bodies, who depend on me for life and for protection. For space, for truth, for healing, for righteous action, and depend, most of all, on me to remember that they are more than just bodies. Because behind each wrinkled anxious squeaky body lies a story, and a family, and a life that is unique and unlike any other. A person, a face, a story, a home, each with their own kitchen tables, shoes, wallets, spaces, jackets, fingers, receding hair lines, wrinkles, mismatched teeth, blood, bones, fears, dreams, loves, lips, words, and hearts. Each a life full of purpose, hope, and meaning, with each bump and bulge and wart, drop of blood and epithelial cell distinctive. As a nurse, I touch more than just a body, I touch a person. I have the privilege of entering their story in a deep intimate way. My challenge is to keep learning and remembering and teaching, that

Naked Hope

with each body I touch, I don't just draw blood or change dressings or help swallow pills, but I touch a body's story and reach a body's heart. In my world, nakedness takes on its own complex identity and definition. I see naked people everyday but in a context completely devoid of normal associations with the word "naked." I don't think of them as "nude." That's an artsy or sexualized form of the body, something that happens in studios or on stages. The people I see and touch are naked. They are stripped of almost every layer that our society values. Their education and job title don't matter; both fund managers and convenience store clerks can have heavy thighs and turkey necks. Without clothes that have been carefully chosen to flatter by drawing the eye away from bodily flaws, most of our competitive advantages and perceived status falls apart. It's hard to project a powerful or unique "personal brand" when your butt is hanging out of a gown and you are wheeling an IV on a pole to the toilet. That is the great leveler. By the time most of the world is done wiping sleep from eyes in the morning, I have stripped multiple strangers stark naked. The world is full of countless morning routines full of faces in front of mirrors brushing on courage for the day, hands digging through dresser drawers searching for just the right outfit to cover it all. In

17

stark contrast, I see countless morning routines full of naked bodies lined up for inspection. What they work so hard to cover up, I promptly scalp right off.

Everyone looks the same in a hospital gown. Rolls and folds hanging unavoidably out the flowing open back. Tissue thin fabric leaves little to the imagination, revealing every bump, bulge, and blemish. It's a common sight in the hospital, two cheeks swinging in the breeze flanked by waving gown strings down the hall, their owner white-knuckled in focus, balancing support from a creaky walker. All stripped of the security, the identity offered by clothes. People are pretty good at hiding inside clothes. Wake up in the morning. Paint on the face full of smiles. Comb out the mess. Button up the questions inside. Zip tight the hurt. Put our best foot forward... only show what appeals. But when they come to me, they are all sick. It's here with me they are stripped, exposed, and vulnerable, unable to hide.

Some days, it's ironic how I am confronted with a profound juxtaposition; I see the spiritual dimension in the middle of rooms filled with naked people. I see people reduced to the most basic form of their humanness. In the Bible, the first things that Adam and Eve do after disobeying God is to realize that they are naked, become ashamed of it, and cover themselves. We are a race that hides our nakedness. We all use fig leaves, fashions, and anything else that keeps people from discovering how pale or frail or disproportionately framed we really are. But this is us. We have arthritic limbs covered with weird rashes. We get love handles and gray chest hairs. Sometimes our eyelids droop or twitch. As we get older, we lose muscle mass and tone, shrink as we stoop, and our abdomen swells.

We all do this, eventually. The naked people I see everyday aren't differentiated by their jobs, incomes, accomplishments, politics, or sense of style. They are simply naked people, with bodies that need care, cleaning, and chemicals. Naked in form, naked in need.

They are also naked in their crisis. It is crisis that has stripped them of the layers of their public identity. It might be their heart or lungs—or both, and a dozen other failing systems as well, like an airliner with all the warning lights and alarms in the cockpit going off at once. It is an existential crisis, in the truest sense of the word, for their very existence is in jeopardy. For most it is also a financial and family crisis as the cost and consequence of their illness is measured and met by everything and everyone in their life. The crisis is emotional and mental and spiritual.

For some, it is the beginning of the end; for others, it is a foreshadow of days that are not as far off as they used to be. They face this crisis in a uniform: a thin gown that was not designed to flatter, issued to everyone regardless of who they are outside this place. In here, they are the army of the naked and sick in the fight of their lives.

I am a progressive care nurse in a small, inner city, Catholic hospital. We serve many who are poor, uninsured, homeless, addicted, or chronically sick—and some who are all of the above.

When I started working here, there were nuns on staff who wore full habits—brown robes and headpieces with ropes around their waists—with cell phones and pagers clipped to the ropes. They roamed the hallways, advocates for the undressed and underprivileged patients. If this hospital were a character, it would be one of these sisters. They had seen it all and had grown a street-wise eye for truth and a formidable crust. They worked as social workers, music therapists, in addition to being spiritual caregivers. These sisters would go fearlessly into rooms with addicts and alcoholics, predators and victims, and get into it with them. They could discern the truth of who these bodies really were, stripped of all their plumage or scarlet letters, naked in their crisis. Because that's what happens in this place: crisis creates an opportunity for patients to confront the truth of who they are, naked and exposed in their humanness.

The naked I see are poor whites, Hispanics, restaurant owners, pastors and priests, gang members, rich people who prefer a Catholic hospital and can pay their bill, Vietnamese and Bosnian immigrants. If the paramedics find a homeless guy collapsed in a snow bank with a blood alcohol content of 1.3, they bring them here. There are a lot of drug seekers and repeaters. There are many who bounce around a network of social service and outreach facilities. They use one and then move on to the next. They find the holes and gaps in the system and both use and fall through them. There are a wide variety of suicide attempts from people in their mid-twenties to those approaching seventy. Some come in with chronic mental disease exacerbated by other physical ailments; they might have diabetes, but because they are also schizophrenic, they forget to take their medication.

My unit is the catch all: anyone who is unstable, no one sure if they will heal or decline and move to the ICU. I don't see healthy people who are in the hospital for normal things (like having a baby, or a collarbone broken in a softball game, or getting tonsils taken out). My patients are sick and in crisis. On any given day, I can have a drug overdose and suicide attempt by a twenty-five-year-old in one bed, a fifty-year-old going through alcohol withdrawal who is delirious and combative, an eighty-five-year-old with renal failure and heart disease, and a kidney transplant patient who's been on dialysis waiting for a donor kidney to become available. Most of my patients are at least sixty, and their bodies are failing. Their illness are largely lifestyle related: eating, drinking, smoking, lack of exercise. Some operate from the disadvantages of poverty, lack of education, and unhealthy culture. Others are successful businessmen who have a sort of cognitive disconnect in how they treat their body. Mortality is catching up with all of them.

And in all of this there is the truth of nakedness. Their clothes or jobs or addresses no longer separate them. They can no longer hide the truth of what they look like, who they are as human beings, and what is wrong with their body and behavior. The truth about these people, like their naked bodies, is not always, or even often, inspiring. About thirty or forty times a day I think, "What am I doing here?"

The answer is I am learning that this is my place. This hospital has shaped my life, and my story is woven through it. I was born in this very hospital, in which I now help and heal the naked and needy. My mom and dad met in this hospital. She was an occupational therapist in the affiliated rehabilitation hospital next door, and he was a recreational therapist. They would meet and pray for their patients. And my dad would pray for—well, for my mom to love him. He would bring his guitar and play for their patients, she would watch, and the love that was born became the beginning of my story here. Five years later, I entered the world in this hospital, a naked and needy newborn myself.

This hospital has shown me the truth about who I am, as well. As much as it maddens me at times, I love working here. I must have dreamer DNA: not only from my parents and their hospital romance, but from my opera-singing grandpa who trekked on expeditions to the North Pole and a Grandma who ran around India in the 1950's and helped to birth babies in the Himalayas. So I can't help it, I was born this way. When I was younger, all these dreams cultured in my cells, like little Petri dishes of idealism. I had grandiose dreams of bringing a cure to AIDS in Africa, of healing patients of dreaded diseases with clever wits and subtle touch, of transforming sad and lonely souls with joy and purpose. I went to college to become a healer, a compassionate hero. I had a lineage, a worldview, a charge to keep. Ponytail high, eager pants on, a silly grin from ear-to-ear, I marched forward with high hopes and mustard seed faith. Give me your tired, your sick, your poor, your hunched-over, and retching masses, I thought. I was going to grow up and be the modern-day Florence Nightingale.

Of course it hasn't worked out exactly like that. Cleaning naked, broken people every day is far from heroic. Not many people look good when they are naked and in need, and the more nakedness and neediness you see, the more you can despair of the human condition. People in their naked natural state can be disappointing. Caring for them can be a disheartening business of not enough money, time, staff, resources, etcetera, etcetera. Politics and personalities color everything, often for the worst. You learn to carefully process the reality of patients and yourself and to appreciate this complex organism that is the hospital.

I've learned a lot about people by seeing them naked. That's what this book is about. Naked hope. Nurses see human nakedness with a unique lens, a vantage point. A nurse is the first and the last person that most of us meet in this world. A nurse wipes and washes and measures the naked and needy infant, fresh and new to the world. A nurse wipes and washes and measures the naked and needy terminal patient, worn and slowly slipping out of the world. A nurse sees and manipulates our most intimate parts under harsh fluorescent lighting, feeds us, fills us with life-giving chemicals, carefully controls everything that flows in and out of us, and listens to our incoherent rants. A nurse sees how you treat your family when they visit, and how they treat you, sees how you respond to pain when you are alone in the dark cold morning, sees how fear keeps you awake through the night. A nurse learns who you really are as a human being.

But as much as the human condition is cause for despair, the news is not all bad. Our instinct is to hide our nakedness, to be ashamed of it. But if we face the truth of who we are, we will find the antidote to shame and despair.

Whether you are a nurse, a teacher, a barista, or a convenience store clerk, we all see the rawness of naked things and struggle to find hope to rise above. Being at the hospital has exposed my nakedness as well as the naked bodies that surround me, but it is in confronting my own vulnerable exposure that I discovered hope. It is in this nakedness that I have found reason to hope. Hope for my patients, and hope for myself.

One

Birth

When I was a new nurse, greener than my scrubs, I would say a simple prayer as I drove to work every morning: "Please God, don't let anyone die because of me today. Amen."

I promised myself that I wouldn't quit for one year, no matter how bad it got. I remember driving into work at the hospital that first year in tears before I even got there, terrified, gripping my steering wheel with white knuckles while I prayed, "Please God, just don't let me kill anyone today." I would cry in the bathroom between patients, I would cry with patients, and I would cry in front of other nurses and physicians. I was a mess. I felt completely incompetent. Everyday I came to work, I felt like I was walking straight into a lion's den filled with the beasts of my own weakness and inadequacy and failure. The weight of dealing with death and addiction and crisis and loss felt too heavy for my little-white-suburban-middle-class

Bible-Belt heart to bear. My decisions everyday had the power to change the course of another human's story, for better or worse, for life or death, and I was petrified.

My bosses made sure I had patients that I could handle and weren't too out of control. I kept repeating to myself what I had learned in nursing school, the "Five Rights" of medication administration: right patient, right medication, right time, right dose, right route. Trying not to fatally screw up (literally), I tried to avoid big problems and big questions and focused on the small things I could control.

Like workers everywhere, I know my commute by heart.

I arrive at the parking structure in the dark, and from my parking spot on the fourth level, I take in the city lights before I get out of my car. Traffic moves slowly along the highways like an illuminated snake. A convoluted network of hallways connects the parking garage to various nodes within the hospital. Through it, the night and day shifts trade places. Nurses, doctors, therapists, and aides are coming or going in a hurry, all dressed in green or blue scrubs. Most days, I skip the sheltered, warm walkway from the parking structure to the main building. I like to brave the elements and walk around the outside of the hospital before going in for the day. I find myself craving a few moments of real, fresh atmosphere, even if it is in the middle of downtown, before tasting sanitized hospital air for thirteen hours. That short, often cold walk helps me remember that whatever happens on my shift, life will go on in this city. Before I give myself to the sick and dying, I feel grateful to be able to move and feel the weather on my skin.

It's usually dark when I arrive and sometimes dark when I walk back up the hill to my car. But as I walk down the hill from the garage, lights from the gardens on the hospital's fifth floor glow like a halo on the old building. I can see it from blocks away as I walk along the outskirts of the business district. Parking lots, offices, visitor lodging, and new additions pile together, filling a whole city block right in the middle of Grand Rapids' Heartside District. Just a few blocks from downtown's best restaurants, clubs, and offices, the Heartside district is a stretch of homeless shelters, missions, and soup kitchens. I pass several street dwellers sleeping on cardboard, guarding whatever fills their shopping carts with one eye. Others are already up, pushing their carts or shuffling toward one of the rescue missions for a free breakfast.

I like this walk from my car to my job. It gets me ready on the way in, and it helps me decompress on the way out.

Once inside the building, I take several different elevators and back hallways through the maze of new and newer additions to this ever-growing hive. Coffee in hand, lunch in a plastic grocery bag, I step onto the elevator for my third floor unit. A ding and the glowing level three light indicates I've arrived. I put my game face on right before the silver doors split open. Sighing, I push my shoulders back, take a deep breath, and step into my day.

Our unit doesn't look like the hospital wards on TV or in movies. Over the last decade or so, research on the most therapeutic and healing environment for the geriatric population has changed the way units like mine are designed. Ours was remodeled into a patient care area just last year, so it still looks fresh and new. Built-in benches line the long hall. Florescent lights have been replaced with warmer, yellow lighting. Local art covers the walls along with several fish tanks, and a fireplace in our family room makes it feel more like a motel than a hospital. Carpet and lamps take the institutional edge off the place. If it wasn't for the cubbies housing computers outside each room and the red, green, and yellow bright light above each door, it could almost pass as a hotel hallway, at least it could at 6:30 in the morning before everyone is awake. In fact, a patients' wife told me the other day it felt like they were staying at a hotel.

But it's hard to hide what we do. The smells and sounds give it away. My nose often catches several distinct odors when I step off the elevator. And I can often tell how my day will go by the sounds that greet me. Muted alarms from cardiac monitors and IV pumps give me the pulse of the place. This relative calm won't last long; by 7:30 a.m., the empty halls will be full of green scrubs, white coats, walkers, and shuffling IV pole pushers.

I have hated needles for as long as I can remember. When I was thirteen, I went to get my ears pierced at the mall. When the first needle went through my lobe, I turned a weird shade of green under the florescent lights. The next thing I remember, I was on my back on the cold tile. Racks of brightly-colored teeny-bopper jewelry were blurry as Brittany Spears music made my head hurt. The piercing place employees were bringing me to after I had fainted. "Breathe, just breathe. You are gonna be okay. It's just a needle, just a little needle. We can't quit now. You want some juice or pop? You poor thing..." There was nothing I could do. My body was reacting to my phobia, and I could not control it. There I was, a sweaty mess on the floor, shoppers all around whispering and staring at the green colored thirteen-year-old girl. I wanted my ears pierced so badly. I was only halfway through, and I would never be able to live it down if I left with only one ear pierced. It took another forty-five minutes for me to recover enough for them to do the second ear.

So when nursing school introduced me to needles, blood, guts, slicing, and dicing, I realized that this just wasn't my thing. I hated nursing school. I decided that I was not cut out for it, and I almost quit on a weekly basis. I felt like I was learning a new language and culture while attempting to memorize every fact that has ever existed about the human body. I would hang over the toilet at 4 a.m. in my dorm room, dry-heaving while nervously getting ready for a clinical training day at the hospital, stomach queasy and knotted with fear and dread. I passed out in the OR, cried in my professors' offices, failed classes, quit classes, retook classes, joined multiple support groups. In fact, I failed a class in nursing school, Nursing Ethics. Who fails ethics? What did that mean? Was I not ethical? Long story short: I had an attitude and didn't feel like spending the money to buy the book. After I got an F on the final exam, I sat down with my professor and cried and begged and pleaded. He just smiled gently and said, "Failure is a beautiful thing."

I stayed an extra year (not by choice), got tutoring, got counseling, tried to get divine help by getting listed in the emails of several church prayer chains, and finally passed my last class my senior year by one percentage point. I was certifiably educated to do this job, but it wasn't a pretty picture. I was too proud and ignorant and hurt to understand what that professor had meant until I started working at the hospital. Every day I felt like I was failing. I was surrounded by death and dying and problems bigger than my passion. Every day I left just grateful if my patients survived. I didn't feel like I was making any sort of difference for anyone.

But the only way through was forward. I had to learn to accept that I couldn't heal every hurt. It was in learning to accept that it was okay that I was not big enough to fix it all that I was confronted with my nakedness. My choice was to either let that failure define and confine me, or let it expose me and move me forward. I had to choose to accept my inadequacy to fix all the broken bodies before me and to remain resilient and eager to learn. Choose to still give each patient my all, everyday, day after day. That became my mantra: try to learn something today, become better at the things I am not good at, don't avoid tasks that I dread. At night I would dream about needles and medication drips and cardiac rhythms and ABG values and arterial line protocols and cardiac arrest code drills. I would wake up in the middle of the night, calm myself down, and resolve to do it again tomorrow.

When I arrive at work, I check in. But again, it's not like it looks on TV. Gone are the days of a noisy central nursing station. Now each nurse pushes her own workstation on wheels, wheeling their computers from room to room as they pass out meds and do their assessments. Everyone carries their own phones, so they page physicians, talk to families with questions, and do their own business from their own mobile station. Different chirping and buzzing can be heard coming from hip pockets as pagers and phones ring up and down the hall. Each noise means something. A call light, a bed alarm, a cardiac red alert, an IV pump empty—all beep at their own pitch, filling the hall with a cacophony of electronic clamor.

What a cohort of nurses we are. Any nurse is only as good as their team, and I think I get to work with the best of them.

"Look, he's mottled to the gills and breathing like a banshee," Susie might say. "You better get up here quick or we're gonna be intubating at bedside." Susie can walk in a room and know within fifteen seconds what needs to happen. As a seasoned intensive care nurse, she has been doing nursing work at this hospital since before I was born. She can smell crisis before it ever hits the door. I often follow her into a room to find stress and fear instantly calmed by her laugh and unquenchable pursuit of answers and healing. Time and time again, she is at the bedside of the sickest of the sick throughout the hospital, fighting for answers and the best possible care for the most vulnerable.

The first time I met Dawn, she was elbow deep in a vicious oozing wound, cleaning pus and stool, smiling and chatting away. Dawn sparkles. And she brings out joy and sparkle from the most difficult and unhappy people in the world.

Connie doesn't quit. Whether it's sixty minutes of trying to get someone clean or five phone calls to a physician to get things right, she jumps into stress like a pool on a hot summer day with passion and conviction.

Patti is a force to be reckoned with. When something goes wrong or someone has a question, you want Patti there. Outspoken and passionate, she is like a momma bear protecting her cubs as she advocates for her patients. There couldn't have been someone better assigned to my training. Short and blonde, I am kind to a fault. Tall, honest, and unafraid to say what she means, she never stops asking questions. I learned to ask questions by watching Patti.

Dee, a fellow charge nurse, deals with sickness and suffering both at work and at home. A diagnosis of cancer in her immediate family left them shaken but not undone. Not naïve to the reality of hardship and heartache involved in chemotherapy and radiation, she grieved and worried, but never let go. She doesn't hide struggle or pretend that nothing is hard, but she is one of the most grateful people I know. Laughter and joy exude from her like suds from an over saturated sponge. In the midst of set-backs and words like "more chemo," she still believes that God is good and big enough to shoulder it all. I heard rumors about her the first day I started. Quite the reputation preceded her: passionate, skilled, articulate, and joyful, always joyful. Rumors couldn't have been truer. Dee isn't just a nurse; she is a healer, an advocate. Her staff and her patients know it. A day with Dee on the floor is always a good day, no matter how stressful or busy things become.

When I get off the elevator, there is desk and a secretary, and when I arrive she is busy typing. The night shift staff gathers by the desk, waiting for us to be ready to relieve them. We gather as a team before the day and go over brief announcements before scattering to get report on our patients for the day. My rounds start right after the charge nurse reports at 7:30 a.m. I get the report from the night shift charge nurse about each patient: what their needs are, who is not doing well, issues with patient care, or complicated pathophysiologies and psycho-social situations. I am in charge of thirty-two patients, some sixteen staff members, and all that happens to that collective group of people during a thirteen or fourteen hour time period. I start my rounds. I walk the circle of the unit all day. Each bed sits in the center of the room, so at a glance, I can see the foley catheter bag hanging from the bar on the end of the hospital bed or check the placement of a BiPAP mask on a patient's face. The cardiac monitor hangs above the bed, so I can also see their cardiac rhythm and vital signs as I walk in the room. I start at room 301 and make my way around the loop to 332 and start another lap. The beds sit parallel to the hallway, so I can walk by, take a step or two inside each room, and quickly survey the equipment and the patient's face. I poke my head into each room, eyeballing the cardiac monitor hanging above each bed, IV drips that are titrating, BiPAP machines, chest tubes, and Foley catheters hanging from bed rails. I can tell by a small monitor beep what room might need more attention. In nursing school, I had a professor challenge me to try to figure out as much as I could about a patient without ever talking to them, looking at a chart, or lab results, so I have fun laying eyes on a complete stranger, lying in a bed, and absorbing as much information about who they are and what is going on in their body just by watching. Watching them breathe, how they move an arm, or grimace with a cough. Looking at the tips of their fingers and the color of their toes or the movement in their abdomen.

Most people will tell you to "Follow your heart. Do what you love. Find your passion." I have come to disagree. The easiest thing in life is to do what you love. But God and my Grandma convinced me to hold my passions loosely, and do what I thought I was meant to do. I grew up hearing her stories, a nurse who made a difference. She was a nurse and an explorer. She climbed the Himalayan mountains as a midwife nurse and saved lives birthing babies in mud huts in the jungles of India. I thought it was in my blood, and I wanted to save the world. I wanted to do something important, to make my life matter, to be like my Grandma. And so, I went against the current of my inclinations, paddling way, way outside of my comfort zone. I did what I was not good at, what I feared, what I dreaded most.

And I discovered that when we are stripped of all that we find comfortable, we find genuine hope. In my case, I found this work, that came so hard to me is where God met me in my weakness and nakedness and birthed meaning and hope. That gives me hope and makes me determined to be as much like Him as possible by meeting other people in their weakness and trying to bring hope and meaning. I'm not trekking mountains and jungles, just walking into work from a parking garage. But like my Grandma, I am learning that for now, I am where I'm supposed to be.

Two

Blood

He was peeing blood out faster than I could put it back in. No one was sure why his bladder was bleeding so profusely, but while I watched, it slowly drained a dangerous amount of blood. I called doctors and specialists and intensive care resources. I slid needles into multiple veins, sucking out more blood to run more tests. I poured bag after bag of someone else's blood into his veins in an attempt to replace what he was losing, but it just wasn't enough. Shades of white grew progressively paler across his face as the morning passed. The first bed change, with all the linens saturated in bloody urine was shocking, but the multiple changes that followed were hard to describe to the physician. His life was draining onto the stark, white sheets in bright, red streams of urine, reducing the volume necessary for life. Hypovolemia is a condition that happens when there is a lot of fluid loss. It can happen through diarrhea, vomiting, bleeding—

anything that drains the body of fluid volume. Like letting all the air out of a tire or stabbing a hole in a waterbed, when volume decreases, pressure drops. As his blood seeped out, he grew as white as the sheets he was laying on, and he was getting weaker by the minute as his blood pressure plummeted. He was still joking with me as I took his blood pressure and stared at a number that is usually not compatible with life: 42/16. Most people would be unconscious. I think he was close, but still fighting at age eighty-seven. Within thirty minutes I was pushing his bed as fast as I could to the intensive care unit, bags of red blood swinging wildly from the IV pole above his head. As fragile as we are, it is a miracle how resilient we remain.

I used to be ridiculously squeamish around blood. More than once, I passed out during nursing school clinicals in the operating room or even just while watching IV starts and lab draws. I have even passed out, hitting the floor hard while attempting to donate blood, unable to tolerate having my finger pricked and seeing that drop of blood ooze out and bead on my finger tip. Blood elicits such a funny response from humans. We see it splattered comically across zombie movie screens or epically spilled in war films. Some people can't stand the sight of it, get pale and pass out. Some have a creepy fascination, while others ignore and avoid it.

Every heart is a little different, but most will beat roughly fifty to ninety times a minute. The average adult body contains roughly five liters of blood, so your heart, when functioning properly, will pump almost all of the blood you own through your whole body once every minute. This rapid circulation is a good thing—it oxygenates your core vital organs, as well as your peripheral extremities—but it becomes a dangerous liability when there is a leak in the system. "Bleeding out" is a phrase used in the hospital to describe a situation when someone literally is losing blood faster than the body or a healthcare team can replace it.

People "bleed out" for all sorts of reasons. One of the most common that we see are the "GI bleeders." An ulcer or diverticuli in the intestinal tract can bleed when irritated. Almost any nurse can smell different pathological processes in feces. I can smell a GI bleed down the hallway. Bloody poop has a very distinct odor. Sometimes it is just a little bleed that can be easily fixed, but I had a patient recently who almost died because of a diverticuli. Bleeding to death from the inside out is a horrifying situation, but it happens all the time.

Another patient came in for fatigue and weakness. He had felt that way for several days prior to his admission. Then he began to notice that his stool was dark and tarry. Since he was stable and only mildly symptomatic, the physician staff scheduled him for testing in the afternoon. But he did not make it to the appointment. They didn't know the exact cause of his bleeding and couldn't until they put a scope up his intestinal tract through a lower gastrointestinal colonoscopy. By mid-morning, his blood pressure was getting low and he began telling the staff that he needed to urgently use the bathroom. Before we could get him up, he had a massive bowel movement in the bed, filled the sheets with bloody stool. An explosion would be a more accurate description. There was blood everywhere. Stool and blood pooled under the bed and a slow dark ooze kept coming. Doctors were paged and units of blood were transfused. Losing that much blood all at once can induce many different complications, including myocardial infarction (a heart attack) or hypovolemic shock. He was close to both. We rushed him to the procedure room and cauterized the bleed, but he almost pooped out his whole supply of blood.

Naked Hope

I see blood everyday. I take blood from people to test it. Every morning, patients in the hospital will endure a rude awakening with a phlebotomist needle in their arm or hand. These morning lab draws determine the plan for the day. Scanning appendages for desirable promising vessels has become second nature for me. I often find myself staring at strangers' arms and hands while in line at the grocery store or paying at a restaurant. I think to myself (and sometimes out-loud), "Wow, now that is a great antecubital! I could stick a 16 gage IV in that vein while blindfolded." But, ironic truth be told, I hate needles. I hate watching the dread fill a patient's eyes when they see the needle and the tourniquet in my hand. Many patients leave with telltale bruising up and down their arm, battle-wounds from days of blood draws and IV starts. But I also know that the blood I take and the IV's I start keep people alive. It's an intimate thing to take someone's blood, a sterilized but strangely intimate process. Gloved up under glowing florescent lights, my blue plastic coated fingers wander up and down arms. Feeling, stroking, pushing, and tapping, I search for the right feel, the perfect spot to slip a needle through layers of epithelial tissue until the flash of bright red blood pops into my syringe. Grown men cry, old ladies scream, and confused patients swing punches, while I pray and poke and suck blood. I am just doing my job, while my patients are stuck, in bed, in gowns, waiting for the next needle to walk through the door.

One day, one of my patients couldn't take it anymore. I am not sure what the last straw that set him off was, because he had been quiet and docile all day. On admission, he was sullen and flat, refusing to talk about his drug and alcohol history. Throughout most of my shift with him, he begrudgingly complied with my requests, let me put fluids in his IV, draw labs tests every six hours, and monitor his heart rate and blood pressure closely. His medical record was full of depression, aggression, and other dramatic psychological encounters and conditions. I have gotten a forced education on how to communicate with volatile individuals (listen much and talk little), and I used that philosophy all day with him. I thought he was making progress. We had several long discussions, and I left the room pretty confident that he was settled and would be amenable the rest of my shift. But not two minutes after I walked out of his room, I heard blood-curdling screams. The first thing I saw as I ran into his room was a spray of blood that he did not seem to be aware of at all as he violently swung a huge arm chair over his head against the seventh floor window. He had pulled out all his IV's, and blood was streaming down his arms and showering the windows as he attempted to bash his way out. I just stood there, dumbfounded, until I just got angry. I remember thinking, this is ridiculous. So, I walked up to him and quite matter-of-factly told him to put down that chair and sit down in bed. I don't think he knew how to respond to me. He stopped mid-swing, chair suspended above his head, blood dripping down, and seemed to snap out of whatever had come over him. Slowly, he lowered his makeshift weapon and sat. Not saying much at all, he let me wipe the blood streams, patch his arms, and calmly clean up the bloodbath. Caring for patients withdrawing from alcohol and drug overdosing is never boring.

Mid-forties and three times my size, he buried his head in that stiff, white pillow and bawled. Broken-hearted from a break-up, as he wept he told me that he had guzzled Drano and yet, surprisingly, didn't die like he had hoped. I sat on the edge of his bed and listened to his tale of woe, engaged and empathetic. I had only been a nurse for about eight months. Fresh off orientation, I was still deliciously naïve. My patient that morning was well over six feet tall and at least 250 pounds, but he seemed small to me as he cried out his story in that hospital bed. I pumped liters of fluids and charcoal through his system to deactivate and neutralize the poison he had consumed. He had IV's going through both arms flushing out his kidneys and stomach. I talked with him quite a bit the first part of that morning. We discussed his life choices, how to cope with stress, and resources that might help. I didn't pay much attention to the woman who slipped in a few minutes after lunch. I was busy with another patient, but as I walked by the room I heard him shouting something that sounded like, "Don't you talk about my momma that way!" This was followed by a blood curdling scream and another shout of, "I'm gonna kill you!"

The next thing I knew, she came barreling out of his room, sprinting for her life with her head back and arms desperately pumping, her screams mixing with his. She whizzed by as I stood frozen and dumbfounded, and a split second later, he lit out after her, stark naked. Gown stripped, arms spurting blood, eyes a little crazy looking, the only thing that I could think was, "He really is going to kill her." Everything froze. People stood at the desk mid coffee gulp, laughs mid-throat, pens mid-stroke, as if God himself had punched a giant pause button. Except for me. To this day I am not sure what came over me. Adrenaline?

Mindless instinct? But before I could stop myself, I found my own feet pounding and arms pumping in pursuit of my crazy patient. My five foot tall, 105 pound, bouncy blonde frame was now on the heels of a huge, bloody, naked man trying to kill someone. I remember wondering as I chased along, all too late, what I would do if, by any chance I actually managed to catch up with him. Throw myself at his naked, bleeding body in a football tackle? Gnaw at his ankles? Hang from his swinging fists?

The hospital unit was laid out in a giant loop. Our comic threesome came back around the nurses station to begin a second lap: the girl sprinting and screaming in the lead, the man barreling along nakedly on her heels, still squirting blood and violently shaking his fists, and then me ridiculously following along, desperately trying to come up with a plan. The staff were fumbling to call for a security team.

I don't know how long our crazy train would have kept going, if one of our male nurses had not heard the chaos, and come around the corner at the just the right time to full-body tackle my naked, bleeding patient to the floor. I stood above them, breathing hard, still wondering what had just happened. Security guards swarmed the floor and carried him still screaming and crying to his room to lock him down in his bed.

As I stood there, panting and staring at the bloody smear on the tile where he had been taken down, I thought about how odd our relationship with blood is. It is the currency of life. Without it, we can't draw a breath or think a thought. In an instant—an accident, an act of violence, a birth gone awry, or a small, burst vessel in our bowel—we can be covered in it and forced to make rational decisions. Then there is no time for squeamishness or prissy niceties. Blood has been the constant that has run through all the varied generations that have walked this earth. It is what we pass on, the river that runs through us to the future. Whether it runs through veins that are young or old, rich or poor, black or white, sane or crazy, my job is to keep it flowing.

Blood is technically considered a "connective tissue" in the medical and nursing world. It connects every system, cell, and molecule you possess. It holds your insides together. You need it to eat, breathe, move, and protect yourself. White blood cells aggressively fight off infection, protecting you from invisible foreign invaders. Hemoglobin is a main component of your blood; it cleans up and carts out the internal trash while carrying in healthy nutrients and necessities. Identity, family, life, and death are in your blood.

When I got home from work last night, my husband pointed to my shoulder and touched a smear of blood imbedded on my white lab coat, left-overs from an eventful day. I could see the face of the man whose blood I touched as I scrubbed my coat clean. Pieces of his story flashed through my mind as I realized how intimate I had become with that stranger, to hold his insides in my hands. As squeamish as blood used to make me, I feel like now I am in the front lines of battle, standing right next to those hemoglobin molecules and white blood cells, fighting to hold you together on the inside. Fighting to keep you connected; connected to identity, to family, to hope, to what matters.

Three

Rainbow

My Grandma taught me how to pray when I was six or seven years old. I remember being mildly disturbed by it. Facedown, arms spread out, she would lay prostrate on the ground. I was a shy and socially awkward kid, so any demonstrative behavior that drew unnecessary attention made me nervous. "Abby," I can still hear her voice, "sometimes when I am talking to God, I am just overwhelmed at how big and great He is, and sometimes the only thing to do is fall on your face. In reverence and awe."

My little brain had quite a hard time digesting that concept. Really? Legs swinging from the edge of a high-back blue speckled chair, I perched, eyes wide with disturbed curiosity, watching. I remember seeing her facedown in her living room, Bible pages splayed open under her gnarled, arthritic hands, crying out to God for our family, for her marriage, for friends in need. And even more than that, she asked big things of Him. Things I thought were quite ridiculous: peace in the world, hope for the hopeless, food for the hungry, healing for the broken. Things I didn't have the guts to dream about, much less ask for. It seemed ridiculous and overreaching. Who does that? But that image of my Grandma is always with me, like a magnet on the refrigerator door of my heart.

Twenty some years later, I have become a woman who makes grown men cry.

Young tough guys, old men who have lived through multiple wars—no one likes needles. Some put on a brave face and force themselves not to flinch, but none of them are indifferent. Some scream, some cry, some moan, some thrash, some punch. I hate to inflict pain, but there are days when I have to stab patients every hour to check lab levels or start IV's or give medicine. It really doesn't matter how logically I explain the medical necessity of the poke or why the IV is important or the consequences of not having medication—knowing why you have to endure pain doesn't prevent the pain.

The patient is at the mercy of my fingertips and skill with a needle. You have to trust the professionalism of the person wearing scrubs and a badge to hold down a part of your body and stab away at it with a needle. The other day, I had to poke a patient three times before I successfully got a functional IV into her arm. Chronic illness has a way of wreaking havoc with the peripheral vascular system, sometimes making it nearly impossible for even expert professionals to obtain IV access necessary for medications to be given. She was already in an extreme amount of pain, and I had to make it worse for a moment to start the IV that would bring the pain medicine to give her relief. She cried through the first two unsuccessful attempts but started screaming and writhing on the third. "I am just so tired of all of this!" was all she could get out in between sobs. I didn't blame her. It was her third time in the hospital in as many months. A debilitating lung disease filled her days with doctor's office visits and hospital stays. Her life was full of needles. And even though she knew I was on her side and that my needle was there to ease her pain, she was sick of the constant stabbing.

I think the only way I can make myself play with the very needles that used to make me sick to think about how the stabbing defuses infections or reverses cardiac arrhythmias or blocks pain. Healing often begins with pain.

Recently, I took care of a woman who had accidentally cut herself with a small kitchen knife. It was an everyday thing, an annoyance that usually brings a few cuss words and a trip to the medicine cabinet for a bandaid. But she developed an infection that spread like crazy, through her entire left arm, wrist to shoulder.

The infection had eaten away layers of skin, and she needed multiple treatments and daily dressing changes. Carefully, I peeled back layers of antibiotic-soaked white, with each inch pulling away as much skin as bandage. I was causing her excruciating pain. It took me almost an hour to pull that dressing off her arm, every little tug was agony for her. But it had to be done. The wound had to be cleaned, the old, dead skin removed so that new, healthy tissue could grow in its place. I tried to make small talk to distract her mind while I wrenched away at her arm, but it was hard for either of us to ignore the pain I was causing. She would breathe heavy, sigh, grit her teeth, and nod when I would stop to give her a break. "Let's just get this done," she would say. Sometimes the only way out of a painful situation is through it.

Sometimes pain is being denied something that you want very badly, even if you shouldn't have it. I remember an obese woman, who had just come off a breathing machine she needed because of her weight. She screamed at me for an hour because she wanted a third meal. Not a third meal that day, but a third meal that hour. Yes, you heard me right. She ate a complete hospital meal and complained that she was still hungry. I felt bad for her and managed to get another brought to her room. She wolfed it down while I went on taking care of the thirty-one other patients who needed attention. Then she hit the buzzer. She wanted another one. It had been only forty minutes since I brought the first, so I told her no. Hearing her screams, visitors in the hallway probably assumed a woman was in labor.

Using my best professional voice, I tried to explain that I couldn't let her eat a third meal within an hour because her blood sugar was too high. Her screaming found another gear. Now the visitors in the hallway probably thought I was torturing her with an electric cattle prod. Other staff started running to the room concerned, expecting a dead body or blood bath, only to see me standing in the middle of the madness, doing nothing. A forty-five-year-old woman was out of control, screaming, writhing, thrashing, and sobbing because I couldn't get her another helping of pressed turkey, mashed potatoes, and jello. What was I supposed to do? I had tried reasoning with her. The truth was, that for her to get better, she was going to have to eat less and lose weight. That was as painful for her as pulling the skin off my other patient's dressing or stabbing a patient over and over looking for a vein. The path to healing often runs through pain.

Sometimes pain is losing things and not being able to remember where they went.

For Jane, life had come to resemble the movie *Groundhog Day*. Her memory loss had her living the same day, over and over again. When she woke up, she knew enough to recognize that she was not at home. But she couldn't remember why she was at the hospital or what was happening. Every day we explained it, and every night she forgot. And so mornings were like waking up in a nightmare: why was she in this place and what was wrong with her? Who was I and the other staff? Why wouldn't we let her go home? We would tell her again and again that it wasn't safe for her to go home alone, that we were trying to find her a safe place to stay, but ten minutes later, she was worried about the same things. Legal complications and safety concerns kept Jane with us for an extended period of time. Putzing and cleaning, she would arrange and re-arrange that hospital room day after long day. She followed the same routine for several long months. Everyone on staff knew Jane. We would all stop in and say good morning, but she didn't remember any of us from one day to the next. We knew everything about her, what she liked, what she didn't like, but every day she felt like she woke up among complete strangers. A bit like a geriatric version of the movie *50 First Dates*, everyday was a restart and repeat.

No family ever came up to visit Jane while she was with us. We were told that several of them had their own serious health issues. Regardless, Jane was pretty much alone. Even though she didn't recognize us from day to day, she became like family to us. We greeted her every morning like a relative. When Christmas came around, there was a present with her name on it under our short plastic tree at the front desk. For many patients in the hospital, holidays are just another day that they aren't healthy; nothing changes. People still get sick and die on Thanksgiving, Christmas, and New Year's. Patients are still hungry and needy and in pain. They check in and out. Life goes on. I was afraid that, despite our present under our little tree, for Jane it would be just another confusing experience, another day she wasn't in the home stored in her long-term memory.

But as Christmas approached, she seemed more upbeat, more hopeful. She started walking in the hallways, smiling, giggling a bit. Her daily struggle to figure out where she was and what was happening gradually eased as the decorations and carols triggered memories and mental reflexes. Bits of tinsel and Christmas cards made an unfamiliar place seem familiar. We had hung stars in her room with old oxygen tubing and found some used red and green garland to make it feel more joyful and festive, and she loved it.

She got to open her present on Christmas. It was just a little wrapped gift under a fake tree, but a lifetime of Christmases tumbled together for her in that happy moment.

It made me think of a line from another movie, *The Shawshank Redemption*: "Hope is a good thing, maybe the best of things, and no good thing ever dies."

Sometimes the path through pain requires persistence.

I remember a patient who looked like death warmed over the first day I met her. Her heart rate was dangerously high, her blood pressure constantly dropping, and she had multiple cancer diagnoses. It was too painful to eat or swallow, and the only thing she could do was try to lie as still as possible and pray that her pain would go away. None of this boded well for her future.

We tried drug after drug to try to fix her heart, fix her blood pressure, fix her pain, but nothing worked. A cardizem drip, an amiodorone drip, fentnyl, dilaudid, dopamine, all without success. Three days of one-on-one nursing care brought no change in her condition. Nurses learn to trust their "gut," to pay attention to their educated guesses and intuition. We all had a gut feeling that things were not going to end well for her. I left for home with a deep sigh, assuming that she would not be there by my next scheduled shift. But she surprised us all.

Her daughter had hovered over the bedside since the moment she came in, not sleeping or eating or leaving for anything other than brief bathroom breaks. We tried to talk her into resting or letting us take over, but she refused. The daughter attended to every one of her mother's grimaces and moans, washing her face, turning her in the bed, moistening her lips. We were in that room all day, for three days, hoping that she would soon see what the rest of us did, that her mom was not going to make it. Physicians and therapists and specialists lined up outside her door and discussed options, but there were no good ones.

But the daughter wouldn't quit. She stubbornly persisted, hoping and praying. First thing every morning, we would see her hunched over the bedrail, softly reading her Bible into her mom's ear. Late at night, after an exhausting day, I passed her room, to see her perched in the same spot, still reading. Not quitting. That third night, I shook my head, wondering if I should say something. But I was too tired to even bother, so I left thinking that I would not see them again.

Monday morning, I showed up to work, and I had to blink a couple of times when I came out of the elevator. The mother was walking in the hallway. She was slow but moving. And smiling. I laughed out loud, glad to have been so wrong. She looked great. Leaning on her walker and using all her strength to lift one foot after the other, she held her head up proud as if no one could tell her that she couldn't walk again.

Naked Hope

I have learned to trust my gut but will never again underestimate the power of persistence to push through pain.

Sometimes, pain is the path to remembering that God always remembers us.

It seemed fitting that it was a rainy day because her day had been gloomy. As if cancer was not enough, she had more tests pending to figure out what else was wrong with her body. She was stable, but the suspense of diagnoses yet to come matched the day outside. She waited in that linoleum covered room to learn her fate. I hate that I don't remember her face. Or her voice. Or even the end of her story. But her path that morning intersected mine in a transcendent moment that affected my soul.

I thought she was doing okay. I gave her the medications on time, colors filling the white pill cup like a set of childhood marbles. But as I passed off that pill cup with the dinner doses, her old finger-tips brushed mine that were not yet calloused, and I stopped to ask one more question: "How are you?"

It was a potentially dangerous conversation to start. As she sat in bed alone all day, wondering and theorizing and worrying, a fear of the unknown had slowly eroded her emotional armor. Answering my question could make her despondent all evening. But her tone was more exhausted than depressed as she replied, "I don't know if I can do this." She wasn't melodramatic but simply honest when she added, "I give up."

Her shoulders slumped, and she broke eye contact. No therapeutic communication technique or workshop on how to comfort despondent patients was going to help me at that moment. I mumbled a lame, "I am sorry," which sounded even worse in real life than it is to read here. I had no idea what else to say, so I tried to be equally honest with her. "I, uh, don't know what to say."

There was a few moments of awkward conversation. Then one of us suggested, and to be honest I can't remember which of us it was, that maybe we should just pray. Saying that to a complete stranger, or having a complete stranger say that to you, is equally dangerous. Some people would rather you offer them rattlesnake than a prayer, but the word had slipped out and hung there in awkward tension. She shrugged, sighed, nodded, and said, "Well, I guess it couldn't hurt."

I hesitantly offered up a nervous prayer. "God, would You help? God, I know You can hear us. God, would You please answer?" Whatever I said, it wasn't any longer or more eloquent than that.

But I had only uttered a few broken sentences when she interrupted me with a shout. "Look!" She started crying loudly. "He didn't forget me."

Startled, I turned and followed her pointing finger. We both gazed upon a huge rainbow, right outside her fifth floor window.

We both sat in the moment. After a while, more of her story came out. She had been a woman of faith. Praying often and with confidence for much of her life, she told me stories about how God had often used rainbows at significant moments of her journey when she needed a reminder of His promise to provide for and protect her. But in the past several years, after many hospital stays, physician visits, and hard diagnoses, she had stopped hearing from Him. Stopped hoping He would answer. Stopped believing that He remembered her. And that day, in that bed, in that room, with my little cup of pills, she was reminded that He never had forgotten. He had been there all along.

There are moments like this at the hospital when I think I finally have come to understand what my Grandma was talking about. Moments when my body might not physically be prostrate but my heart and soul find themselves falling face down. Holy moments when I am reminded that I am a part of something bigger: bigger than myself or my nursing career, bigger than any pain or seemingly hopeless story. More often than not, this happens as I watch my staff live and love and work around me. Rainbows don't always appear, but the real stories of those who live and die around me constantly bring my soul to its knees.

Four

Skin

How would a quadriplegic commit suicide?

It's a horrible question, but I wasn't asking out of perverse curiosity. I was really trying to understand how my patient, paralyzed from the neck down, could manage to take his own life. The answer was that he couldn't—but not for lack of effort. With nothing but his teeth, head bobs, and awkward jerking of his arms from the shoulder joints, he had somehow managed to twist a telephone cord around his neck. It was a creative noose, but of course he couldn't raise himself high enough to fall far enough to do enough damage. Despite his determination, his body wouldn't cooperate in its own destruction.

Now he was here, and while I didn't look down on him in judgment, I looked down to appraise his health. He was red. His skin was red against the white hospital sheets, and so was everything else: red hair, red eyes, red neck (the horizontal lines left by the phone cords were an even darker shade of red across his neck). Red blotches pockmarked his red face. In addition to his paralysis, he was suffering from a skin disease. I began my clinical workup, my cold hands all over his warm skin, feeling his disease between my fingers, touching his troubled flesh. It would hurt, if he could feel it. I stripped the gown from his sweaty skin, and then I bathed him, from red head to red toe. He was stiff, immoveable in body and in spirit, keeping me shut out of his world even as I washed every inch of his skin. I asked but couldn't understand the story of his body.

Garbled words tumbled from his mouth. At first, they were as meaningless to me as nonsense syllables from a Dr. Seuss book, but his eyes were fluent. They were full of hate—not at me personally, but at my existence and presence as someone who was keeping him alive. If the eyes are windows to the soul, his loathed life. He was afraid of spending another day trapped inside a broken body. He was serving a life sentence in solitary confinement, unable to move his own limbs or speak to the people he saw outside the windows in his cell.

Over the course of that day, I got better at understanding both his eyes and his words. I'm pretty sure that he was pissed off when I first walked into his room and threw open the dark shades. The stark, white surfaces were bathed in sunlight as he glared at me. My cheerful chatter clearly irritated him. If looks could kill, he would have been hurling daggers at my face as I smiled and chirped about all the things I had planned for his day. He protested with low, moaning syllables. I leaned over him, putting my ear a hair's width from his red lips. I listened, and asked him over and over to please repeat himself as I tried to make sense of each painfully formed word. It was like learning a new language, and over the hours, I learned to make sense of bits and pieces. He was frustrated that I didn't catch on more quickly, and time and again, he would give up even trying to communicate, retreating back into the silence of his cell. But we made progress. By the end of the day, I could at least get the gist of what he said.

As I touched his red skin, I wondered when he last felt love. An angry red quadriplegic man with severe expressive aphasia, alone in his thirties. How long had it been since he felt a loving touch? When had he last felt at home somewhere, felt seen and wanted? Did he feel forgotten, as prisoners often do? Who remembered what he was like before? Who cared? Who valued him as a human being?

As I watched his stiff, angry, reactive, red body slowly relax that day, I wondered if I was giving him more love than he had felt in years. He was considered a hopeless case; barring some miracle, he would spend the rest of his life surrounded by and absolutely dependent upon workers paid to care for him. His skin condition led me to believe that they did not bother to touch and wash him much. Did they make any effort to listen to his garbled speech, to read the thoughts in his eyes? Could I, an unfamiliar woman in a hospital giving him a bed-bath, be providing the most human and humane experience he had known in a long time? There was no way he could tell me.

Because he was so flinty, I was determined to smile. Two stubborn people spent the day dancing. I wanted to give him hope, to be hope for him. I could not make him walk again, but I could embody the truth that God's love can reach the prisoner in the deepest dungeon. His body was only the outer wall. He had built an inner wall of bitterness around his heart. I could not free him from his cell, but I could visit and give him hope that love could be had and given through its bars.

I thought I saw him reaching through those bars when I bounced into his hospital room the next morning. His red lips formed a slight and awkward smile in his red face.

Making conversation, I mentioned a movie I had seen on TV recently, and he responded. Leaning in, I gathered that he had seen it too and liked it. I asked him what kind of music he liked. It took some effort back and forth, me asking if I had understood and he correcting me, but I gathered that he liked Prince (or "The Artist Formerly Known As Prince," or whatever he calls himself). I'm not a Prince fan, and I told him. All the sudden, we were having a good-natured argument about music, and I learned what his laugh sounded like.

I washed his inflamed skin again, and he stopped hiding in the corner of his cell. By the end of the day, he was smiling as we bantered about bands and TV shows. Once I learned to understand his halting speech, I found that he was clever and funny. I would have never known if I hadn't tried so hard to make contact.

He was one of those patients whose faces and stories I will never forget. It's odd how connected we can feel to someone after only a couple of days. As I cared for his body, I came to care for him. His limbs were limp, his skin was diseased, his mind had been depressed and self-destructive. I knew that once he left that room, I would probably never see him again. But I wanted him to feel valuable because he was valuable. The gift that I could give him was hope that people could see him as a person, not just a patient or a problem.

The next day he was discharged from the hospital to an outpatient therapy center for the severely depressed and actively suicidal. As he got ready to go, his big, red fingers clutched my little white hand in a death grip. I leaned in and whispered, my lips touching his red ear, "You are going to make it. You are worth it. You have so much to offer. I won't forget you." He turned his head, and spoke into my ear. It was a few sentences, and he repeated them several times. After a minute or two, I thought I understood the words, but they seemed out of context. What I thought I heard him say was, "All I really need is to know that you believe. No need to worry, no need to cry, make you happy when you're sad. Yeah, I would die for you."

This took a couple of minutes, and with the attendants waiting, there was no time for one of our halting conversations. I gave him my best smile one last time, and pried his hand from mine as they wheeled the gurney to the elevator.

As I laid in bed that night, his red skin and red face on my mind, I was sure that those last sentences must be some sort of a quote. They were too out of context and repeated too many times to be conversational. I got up, and flipped open my laptop. I hadn't written them down and couldn't recall them exactly, but I was sure about the phrase, "I would die for you." I googled that and added a few other phrases I remembered. After clicking through a few results, and reading through a page, I found what he had said. They were lines from a song by Prince, the singer he liked and I didn't. He was telling me something and teasing me at the same time.

No need to worry
No need to cry
...
Cause you, I would die for you, yeah
Darling if you want me to
You - I would die 4 U
...
Make you happy when you're sad
...
All I really need is to know that
You believe
...
Yeah, I would die 4 U, yeah

Darling if you want me to
You, I would die 4 U
Two, three, four you
I would die for you

I had washed the inflamed skin of a suicidal quadriplegic. He had hated me for trying to draw him out of his bitterness and depression. We ended up arguing about music, like any other two human beings. We had conversed and connected. I laughed and cried in front of my laptop as I finally realized what he had been trying to tell me.

Everyone loves Florence Nightingale. I do as well. I have always pictured her romantically wiping a handsome soldier's brow while her white red cross cap pristinely rested atop her head. However, I recently started reading her work *Notes on Nursing*, published in the late 1800's, and found that I have a completely different picture of who she really was, and I like her even more. She was a spunky nurse who was passionate about her patients and who was not afraid to get dirty. I read this quote from her *Notes on Nursing* this week:

Naked Hope

"Every nurse should keep this fact constantly in mind, for, if she allow her sick to remain unwashed, or their clothing to remain on them after being saturated with perspiration or other excretion, she is interfering injuriously with the natural process of health just as effectually as if she were to give the patient a dose of slow poison by the mouth. *Poisoning by the skin is no less certain than poisoning by the mouth—only it is slower in its operation.*"

I know she was referring to literally washing the physical skin on a body, but I think it is true figuratively as well. My patients get judged for their skin every day; diseases, disabilities, and defects. Judgement that slowly poisons with depression and despair. We all slowly poison each other when our seeing stops at skin level. I was able in those few hours with my patient to wash his skin of that poison; let my words of kindness and compassion wash away the layers of rejection that had built up on his skin.

My patient that day was not an inert, red body. He might not be able to feel his limbs, but he felt—he had plenty of time to feel and think and plan. That's what amazed me about his suicide attempt. How long had he planned it? How long had he waited for just the right opportunity, when someone would position him in just the right proximity to a telephone and leave him alone long enough for him to use his teeth and bob his head? How much time and effort had that taken? He did not want to be a mere spectator, watching life from a prison window. He wanted to engage the world outside his body. He needed help every day of his life, but he also needed hope that people could see him, not just his body. For a couple of days, while he was naked and angry, I tried to be that hope for him.

Like so many of our patients, I don't know what happened to him after he left our hospital. The health care system is vast and complex and compartmentalized by confidentiality laws. Every shift I have brings new faces with urgent needs. But he helped teach me that no matter how broken the body, inside are men and women who can remember the lyrics to their favorite songs.

Look beyond the skin to see the man within.

Five

Dead

Our culture has an odd relationship with dead bodies. Whenever we can manage it, death takes place in hospitals and hospices, where most of us don't see what happens to the body. They are professional spaces, and despite every attempt to make them seem homey with sofas, soft colors, and a watercolor or two on the walls, we have no reason to be in these rooms except to visit a dying relative or friend. The spirit departs, we say our goodbyes, and then leave the professional space. Professionals deal with the body, which we don't see again until it is dressed and coiffed in the casket.

I am one of those professionals. In fact, I am the first in the chain that leads from the deathbed to the memorial service.

I deal with death and dying and end-of-life issues almost every day. Most of my patients die from things that make them ineligible for organ donation, so we don't usually have to hurry to get them to a donation surgical team. After the family has finished saying its goodbyes, we prepare the body to leave the room. We take out all the IVs and wires, remove the catheters, and wash the body. There is a specific odor that develops when someone dies. Once the organs stop exchanging oxygen, a very particular biological process goes into action. The lack of oxygen transfer also mottles the skin. There is rapid color change. Death has a look as well as an odor. If someone has been dying for a long time, they get diaphoretic (sweaty), and the whole room is filled with a pungent smell.

Then it is time to get the cart. So I call security, grab another nurse, and head downstairs. Like all hospitals, the Midwestern Catholic hospital where I work has grown wings and additions over its lifetime, but where we need to go is in the core of the complex, in the basement of the original building. Coming out of the elevator, we head down the hallway to a door directly opposite from the administrative offices, labeled only, "Suite 200." Someone from security is there to unlock it for us; not just anyone can walk into the morgue.

Inside Suite 200 are two big, stainless steel, restaurant-sized refrigerators. The security officer unlocks one of them, and inside is the cart we have come for. It is a heavy, steel contraption from the 1980's. On top is a frame covered with a white tarp, stretched taught, that can be lowered to create a boxy tent. It takes two of us to push it and steer it, and while the security officer holds the door, we grab hold of the cold steel bars and roll it out of the fridge and out of Suite 200.

There are offices right across the hallway from the morgue. The administrative staff inside them knows why a security guard and two nurses went into the door across the hall, and they watch us wheel the cart out. We all have our jobs to do, and the emergence of the cart probably sets some administrative tasks in motion, although I have no idea what sort. While the administration is as committed and compassionate as the nurses, and their office is full of busy tasks all aimed at the healing and benefit of my patients, they interact with the patients in a very different way than I do. In a way, it is more distant, since they don't touch and smell and clean them. On the other hand, they handle finances and family and facilitate everything so that I can do my job. I am struck by the irony that, even though these offices exist solely for them, many patients will only enter this hallway or be exposed to those who work behind the scenes on their behalf, riding on this cart.

As we pass by the offices, the kitchens, and the other parts of the hospital that patients never see, everyone knows what the cart means. And because of our direction of travel with it (going downstairs), they know that we will be returning shortly. There is no way to be discreet; there is no back way, no hidden staff-only route back up to the patient rooms. We push and wrestle the cart through public areas—elevators, lobbies, offices, waiting rooms—full of staff and patients, family and other visitors. We are conspicuous; apart from its size, the cart is noisy. The thirty-year old wheels wobble and squeak on the polished tile floors, and the frame creaks and clangs, warning people to step aside and make way.

The first few times that I pushed the cart, I felt subdued and self-conscious enough to not want to talk. But to be honest, fetching the cart is a part of a regular working day. While the other nurse and I navigate the hallways and elevators and people eye the cart with equal measures of curiosity and dread, we have to stifle our impulse to carry on a normal conversation. We don't want to be seen making small talk or laughing while we bear the cart. And so we avoid eye contact, although most look away when they see us coming. The cart creates a wave of silence as it moves through the hospital, an eye-dropping hush falling on all who spot it. The most awkward moments are on the elevators, when visitors are trapped with the cart and us. They stare at the current floor indicator lights even more intently than normal.

As we emerge from the elevator onto our floor, I know that this cart is an unwelcome sight to patients in the adjoining rooms, so I usually send someone ahead to close all the doors and clear the hallway in front of us. Like a fire drill, we go as fast as possible, hauling toward our destination. But the faster we push it, the louder it squeaks and creaks and clangs, and for the other patients the rapidly-closed door followed by the noise passing by must be weird. Some of them figure it out, and ask the next nurse they see who died. But we are trying to be quick and careen around the corner into the room and shut the door behind us, answering no questions.

Two are not enough for what comes next, so I call for a couple more staff. Sometimes the body has been there for a while. When someone dies, the muscles all relax. Without muscle tension, the distribution of weight changes—they become "dead weight"—and it takes four nurses to transfer the body to the cart. We heave-ho on the count of three.

Flat on the top of the cart is a big, white, zip-lock bag. It's wide open, and we transfer the body onto it, and then zip it closed. Sometimes, the bag is too big. Other times, the people are so big that we have to work hard to close it, like an overstuffed suitcase.

Then we raise the shrouded frame, enclosing the deceased in a white tent. Earlier we had put a tan-colored ID tag on the toe with a rubber band, and pinned an identical tag to the gown. The third tag goes onto the tent frame, and it's time to leave the room.

I send someone out to clear the hallway and close the doors again, and then we reverse the trip. We squeak and clank and we push and pull through the twists and turns. But this time our encounters with patients, family and staff are more uncomfortable than awkward. The halls and elevators are quiet, and people look away. As we head back the way we came, our direction of travel leaves no doubt that we bear a dead body through the houses of healing. And yet, outside the silent zone around the cart, activity continues. Staff members talk in offices, printers spit out paper, phones ring at nurses' stations. Someone's story has ended, but others go on. In the rooms and surgical suites, other patients contend with the frailty of their own bodies, fighting to avoid a ride on this cart.

Naked Hope

As I steer the cart around the corners, I feel the irony
of this task in this familiar place. These are the same halls
and lounges and elevators that I frequent every day. At
any other time I am talking on my phone, or discussing a
patient, or laughing and making plans for the evening. But
now I come bearing death. Perhaps this was the same
route that the patient traveled to get to their room, and
now I am escorting them on their final passage back down
it.

Sometimes, I reflect on the strange and sacred nature
of this moment. I was with this patient during their final
hours. I helped them to go to the bathroom, I met with
and comforted their family, I watched their last breath.
And now I am pushing them as dead weight down to the
morgue. I may have only known them for a few hours, but
I was with them at the end. And now I'm escorting them
through this intimate passage to whatever comes next. It's
a weird privilege.

In the movies there are scenes of somber reverence as
a fallen warrior is put onto the funeral pyre while the
bagpipes play, or as the pharaoh is carried down into the
lower passages of his pyramid, or as the ship containing
the dead sails over the horizon. This seems so banal by

comparison: a near-stranger wheeling them on a squeaky cart past the gift shop.

After we get through all the hallways, past a patio and garden with sunlight, the security officer makes me sign a logbook, with a running list of names of those who have made this final passage. The outer door and the fridge are unlocked. The cart is wheeled in, and it's wheels are locked in the cold space, with the deceased bagged and tagged inside.

Our gloves are blue—blue gloves on a white cart—and I peel them off. There is no sink in the morgue, so I do my best to clean my hands with an alcohol wipe. As I walk away from Suite 200 and back up through the passages to living patients, I am no longer the cart-bearer. But their scent, the smell of their dead body, clings to me.

The phone on my hip is already going off. There are other patients with needs, other problems to solve, other conversations to jump into. And that's what I do, as I leave Suite 200: jump right back into the land of the living. I have another somber memory, but no time to process it or make any sort of gesture. Housecleaning is stripping the bed and making the room ready for whomever is next.

In the back of my mind, as I tighten a tourniquet around another arm to draw blood, I wonder about the dead cart passengers' story, their family, how their whole world is now upside down, while mine keeps on like nothing ever happened. It's an honor. An honor and a privilege to be a part of someone's dying process, to enter into such a sacred part of their story for a few minutes, hours, or days. It is with pride I say that I am a dead-cart-bearer.

Six

Grace

Each of her thighs weighed more than my whole body. Like giant drumsticks, massive piles of flesh hung on her bones. Years of unhealthy eating habits, lack of exercise, smoking, and depression had coated her arteries with disease encrusted plaque, killed off healthy lung tissue, and invaded her body with more fat tissue than good muscle tissue. She was slowly killing herself. Her body structure could no longer support its own weight. Her eyes bulged, her chest heaved, and each breath was an effort as she suffocated under her own flesh and her systems shut down. She had lost her independence with her inability to walk or care for herself. Her fat had become a prison, with the walls closing in.

Most of us react, almost involuntarily, to this picture. It's hard not to feel pity, sprinkled with judgment. It's impossible to hide three hundred pounds of excess adipose tissue. All of her ailments on inglorious public display. We see her problems before we see her. We think that we know her and what's wrong with her before we look her in the eye. It seems obvious: addiction, lack of self-control, and laziness are written in the rolls of her abdomen for all to read. We suspect that buried somewhere in there are emotional issues, manifesting in these obvious physiological symptoms.

I am not immune to these thoughts. But judgment is not my job. So I tried to have a normal conversation, even to get her to laugh. But I could see dread in the constant shifting of her eyes and the hesitancy in her voice. She was waiting for my criticism, my passive-aggressive condescension, my damning with faint praise. She had heard it all before.

She knew she was fat. She felt it everyday. She knew she was sick. She felt it every time she struggled to breathe against the weight of her body habitués. We didn't have to tell her anything; she saw the judgment in our eyes, heard it in our tone, in our questions. And still, almost everyone she met felt the need to point it out, to remind her that not only was she morbidly obese, but also that she needed to hurry up and do something about it—or else.

But if anyone made the effort to read between the rolls, they might have seen shame, fear, hopelessness, loneliness, and rejection. Yes, her pathologies had put her in that hospital bed in front of me. So had so many others who were too thin, too old, too nervous, too addicted, too weak, too proud, too distracted, too lazy, too ignorant, too driven, too sexually active, too poor, too busy, and unlucky enough to be in the wrong place at the wrong time.

As I bustled about her bed, it occurred to me how lucky I was that no one could see my sins. My thighs might not weigh 200 pounds apiece, but everyday my mind, body, and spirit willingly consume just as much—if not more—junk as she did. Her consumption manifested itself with visible consequences, while my thighs never shared my secrets. But at least she confronted and owned her problems. She had no choice but to talk about and cope with her pains and failings and sins. I often wonder what people would think of me if my weaknesses were written on my body for all the world to see. What if all my self-doubt, self-centeredness, greed, anxiety, and bitterness bulged from my face like tumors? What if all my remorseless emotional cruelty and negligence were exposed to passing children on the sidewalk, who could point at their moms and ask in too-loud whispers, "What's wrong with that lady?" My heart has been and sometimes still can be coated with sins every bit as deadly as the plaque in her arteries.

I am lucky, although I'm not sure that I'm blessed: no one knows my diseases, except for me. Inside, I am every bit as unhealthy as she. My thighs might as well be 200 pounds for all the good it will do me for eternity. I am frightened by how quickly I rush to judge others thighs without being willing to see the obesity of my own soul.

Everyday, patients arrive in my hospital because they cannot physically care for themselves any longer. Their bodies have accumulated too much damage through years of abuse and neglect. Most diagnoses boil down to that. Obesity, diabetes, peripheral vascular disease, hypertension, lung cancer, coronary artery disease—the list could go on for another two pages—a tragic cascade of poor choices. A sad parade of smokers and drinkers and drug abusers. We pour all the money and skill and passion we can into patching them up, only to see them leave and fall back into the old patterns.

I ended this week absolutely exhausted. A patient had been admitted, and we spent sweat, blood, and tears mending what he had broken. Morbidly obese, he had stopped taking the medications for his heart and his diabetes, and he had done nothing for a year other than furniture surf and eat take out food. He had fallen and been too weak to get up, so he was left lying on the floor in his own excrement until some friends found him two or three days later and called an ambulance. By the time we got him, his skin was peeling off in layers from wounds he got from the fall. His blood pressure went dangerously low from dehydration, and his kidneys had almost completely shut down from a condition called rhabdomylosis (result of muscle tissue death and breakdown in the body). I paged doctors and nurses and specialists, I spent hours carefully titrating drips and calculating urine output, and I doused him in buckets of soapy water in an attempt to clean years of filth that had worked into his flesh. A team of us spent long days doing everything in our power to heal his body. After a week of this, I learned that he had been in for something similar the year before. The staff had cleaned him, released him, sent him home on the path to wellness—and he had not changed a thing about how he lived his life. As I worked in his room, I listened in as he told his friends he had no intention of going to therapy or working to get better. He was determined to just get home and back to his "normal" life. I stopped as I overheard this. My body was sore and my eyes were heavy after running around all day trying to just keep him alive. I stood there, the nurse in scrubs, ignored as he chatted with his buddies. I wondered, not for the first time, how I was supposed to respond as a caregiver to patients who are self-destructive. How do I keep fighting for patients who can't or don't even want to fight for themselves? How should I treat patients who will walk out my doors and promptly undo everything we worked so hard to achieve?

It's a privilege to be a healer who always believes, always hopes, always sees opportunity, and always fights to give broken bodies a chance—for goodness sake to at least give them the chance—to heal. I'm honored to have the opportunity to invest in the health of the lives entrusted to our care. I take pride in doing everything in my power to set people up to succeed and enjoy a healthy body, mind, and spirit. I know that it is naïve to believe that every body I touch will choose healthy habits or that sadness and addiction will be overcome by truth and goodness and hope. But that isn't up to me. I am simply responsible to give care, to value each life, and to impart wisdom and a reason to hope. I do this because each created life is sacred, from conception to death. I am called to promote and defend human dignity. God called me to see Himself in everyone I serve.

The nuns who helped start our hospital can be traced back to an earlier group of nuns who helped the famous Florence Nightingale. They established hospitals in the poorest of the slums in inner cities around the world. They healed those who had no money or prestige, who had no resources or worth to society. They didn't serve to be heroic but because each life is worth it. When I started working at this hospital, nuns were still a dominant part of the atmosphere. Their presence was a constant visual reminder that our pills and skills are not enough, that each broken body is not a dysfunctional pile of cells and chemicals, but a person intentionally created with a purpose. The *Ethical and Religious Directives for Catholic Health Care Services* are

> "grounded in the conviction that each human person possesses intrinsic worth simply by virtue of his or her existence as a human being. This is not merely a matter of belonging to a highly evolved biological species. Men and women possess inherent dignity precisely because they are made in God's image (Gen. 1:27). Our God is a personal being, and so every human being is a who, not a what, a someone, not a something."

My resources and my time will always be limited. Sometimes it feels like a waste to pour all we have into a body that doesn't give a damn about itself, but each broken, angry drunk who comes in for the fifth time this month deserves that dignity. Our faith tells us that this is exactly what our God did for us.

We all have a choice. It is my choice to look beyond the two-hundred-pound thighs to see the sacredness and dignity of a real person—yes, who has real problems. My job is to give each of my patients an opportunity to choose to be healed. I can't choose for them, but I can partner with them, support them, advocate on their behalf, and help them be able to make the best choice possible. That doesn't mean always smiling and holding hands and trying to make people feel better. Often, that means serious talk, honest feedback, or hard questions. But at the root of it all, I'm all in with the nuns who came before and still surround me: everyone deserves a chance to change, and we are charged by the Creator to see through layers of fat and fear and hopelessness to help his wayward children hope again.

I started running soon after I became a nurse. I was never athletic. I hated anything that made me sweat. But

Naked Hope

within months of starting my first real nursing job, I had to start running out of anger and frustration and disillusionment. I was angry about the lack of resources for people who have nothing, and I was angry at people who wasted what resources they do have on alcohol and cigarettes. I was angry at the government for creating such a nasty mess of insurance and healthcare. I was angry at my own people, the Christians and churches who would not reach outside the doors of their safe little buildings to actually touch sick and dying people in need. Most of all, I was angry at God for not answering when I asked Him to miraculously heal the sick bodies I fought for day after day. So I started running to process my anger. I would run trails though the woods and yell. As I went, I saw the faces and replayed the stories of dying patients, of bodies I helped save, of bodies in pain, of bodies covered with disease. I could not forget their names. My hands would remember the contours of their faces while my feet pounded the trail. Diagnoses and diseases scrolled through my head like CNN headlines while I pumped my arms and gasped for breath between angry sprints. Late at night, after a long, hard shift, and early in the morning before going in for the day, those whose life blood had run through my fingers would keep me company as I hammered the pavement.

A couple things happened when I started to run. I realized that I could run. I certainly wasn't Olympic race material (ha ha), but my feet moved in a mostly coordinated rhythm. I think that yesterday alone, I walked fifteen people to the bathroom who can't walk well enough to go to the toilet by themselves. So I have that going for me. And I realized that I can run whenever I want. What a privilege it is to have a healthy body, feet and legs and bladder and bowels that function. I am so grateful that I can move and so blessed for these taken-for-granted functions. With that gratitude came a sacred hush, a healthy awareness of the fragility of my own life. Genetics, grace, and a praying Grandma have kept me from two-hundred-pound thighs, cancer, addiction, drugs, and much more. An appointment with paralysis and tragedy could await me the next time I drive to the grocery store.

Life is sacred, and life is fragile. Watching patients struggle as they lose their most basic body and mental functions has only made me realize how much I have to celebrate. I refuse to live in fear of what might happen, but I want to live with constant joy for the good things—little and big—that I have. I choose to enjoy each day as a good gift from a good God. I haven't earned any of this, but I know that it has been given to me. I will treasure all this in my heart.

My patients have changed me. My angry rants and screaming matches with God on the trails slowly turned into desperate cries. Desperate cries that started sounding suspiciously like prayers. Prayers for grace. For the broken naked ones I touch, for the broken nakedness in me.

Seven

Breath

Our lives begin with a breath. You spent your first seconds desperately sucking in oxygen with a shriek, squeak, squall, or squeal as your baby lungs filled with air for the first time. Life and hope entered your little limbs with that first breath, just like it has for everyone who came before you.

Our lives end with a last breath. There is a moment of sacred stillness that hushes all when a last breath lets go of clinging lungs and lips, a moment infused with mystery that floats gently above a newly motionless frame built of bone and flesh. And then there is a wait, a queasy, wondering wait where everyone stops breathing for a second to watch that heavy chest for any flicker of movement, watching, waiting, wondering if it will rise again.

Some bodies die out of the blue, stop breathing suddenly. Some bodies have been working on dying for a long time when they finally reach their last breath. But even though no death is the same, there is a moment that is universal. Transcending all race and culture and history and personality. A last breath, a last exchange of oxygen-rich molecules with hemoglobin-carrying red blood cells for a release of carbon dioxide. A last exhale of life. When a body dies and lets out its last breath, an eerie stillness settles over bones that once creaked and lips that once laughed and eyes that once shone. Everything looks the same, but in one breath that complex body-system of cells and membranes that marry flesh and spirit becomes simply a pile of skin and bones, silent and empty. Pink, tender personhood becomes stiff, still stone.

Death has a way of bringing his friends with him when he comes: anger, doubt, despair, fear. One can't but help breathing them in as they fill the air around a deathbed. I breathe them in just as much as my patients and their families. I know what death looks like. I can see him coming, sometimes from a mile away, by the look of an eye or the color of skin or the smell of sweat. And I have to decide, when I see him sneaking around, how to respond. How to take a deep breath full of fear and exhale, exchanging that fear for faith, letting out a huge exhalation of hope.

The act of breathing is quite a multifarious process. A complex coordination of ventilation and oxygenation pressure systems and positive and negative ion exchanges. You breathe in oxygen, and it travels down through your trachea and into smaller passages called bronchi. Those bronchi keep branching, smaller and smaller, into airways called bronchioles and end in little, thin sacs called alveoli. At this tiny molecular level your red blood cells absorb oxygen and release carbon dioxide that travels back up the same passages and out into the atmosphere. Inhale a substance and exchange and create another, filling the air around you with something different than what you took from it. Sitting with bodies and families as they breathe their last, I enter into this cycle in a different way. I don't just give morphine or draw blood or measure output, but as a nurse, I have a front row seat in this sacred exchange. When hopelessness hangs like heavy droplets in the air surrounding bodies in crisis, my job is to breathe that deeply into my lungs, exchange it somewhere in the complex passages inside my body, and exhale hope and peace instead.

When people die, or are trying to die, their breathing pattern is one of the best indicators of just how much time they have left. Agonal breathing—loud and raspy, irregular and labored—tells me every time. I hear death in how fast, or sometimes how slow, that tell-tale sign develops. The average healthy adult respiratory rate at rest is fourteen to eighteen breaths per minute. You breathe in and out eighteen times every minute of every day without giving it a second thought. Subconsciously, the rhythm is hardwired into your body: inhale oxygen, exhale carbon dioxide. Again and again, with little or no effort or conscious awareness. When death comes around, your body has to fight as hard as it can just to keep breathing. All your other peripheral organs begin to shut down to conserve and focus your energy and effort on keeping that exchange going. Fight to inhale oxygen, and fight to push carbon dioxide back out. Once you have seen it, you know all too well how to recognize it: the sight of the sunken cheeks, the blue mottled pattern crawling up the legs, and —most ominously—the sound of lungs laboring to keep going. Each inhalation and exhalation requiring everything.

Even as a trained professional, sometimes I feel helpless watching this process. I know that I cannot always stop death. No matter how much passion, love, skill, or technology I bring to my job, sometimes it is not enough to halt tragedy. Sometimes I breathe in a little too much and have a hard time breathing out something new. Sometimes the hopelessness and despair are overwhelming. Sometimes I find that the exchange goes the other way. Sometimes I draw hope and healing from the naked ones around me.

I tried to help Fran die, but she wouldn't let me. Fran had come in the week before with liver problems but had gone home. But she came back on her ninety-ninth birthday, right after the party. She had been feeling great, eating birthday cake and ice cream. But when she suddenly couldn't get up off the toilet, her family called an ambulance and brought her to me again.

Your liver is a miracle. It would be hard to live without any of your major organs, but the liver is near the top of the list. It does hundreds of tasks, but most importantly, it filters out toxins from the blood. If it is not working then all sorts of crud and poison build up in the bloodstream and spreads throughout the body. The outward sign of a malfunctioning liver is jaundice, as the toxins reach the skin and give it a yellow hue.

Fran was jaundiced, but even with bright yellow skin, I still recognized her. The gastroenterologist note in her chart read: "ischemic liver." Stones had built up in the bile duct of her liver and were preventing the liver from doing its primary job. In fact, they were cutting off the blood supply to the liver. The diagnosis indicated that there were too many stones to remove surgically.

So the physicians tried putting a drain in her liver to clear some of the toxins. But it wasn't enough to keep up, and within two hours after they surgically inserted the drain, her body shut down. She became obtunded, or unresponsive. Her body shook with violent chills (we call them rigors) and her blood pressure plummeted to 50/20 —a life-endangering number. At 50/20, not enough blood is getting pumped to the vital organs. Blood carries oxygen, so 50/20 means that the major organs—the brain, liver, lungs, kidneys, etc.—are being starved of oxygen (we call it lack of perfusion).

I was the charge nurse on the floor that day. When the nurse who was working closely with Fran called me to the bedside to help, I immediately called the team of intensive care resource nurses to help manage the situation. Three of us worked on her. One of us ran to get medicines, and one of us explained to the family what was going on inside Fran's body while busily hanging IV bags and inserting IV needles into her yellow arms. One of us was on and off the phone with multiple physicians, calling out different orders. Machines beeped, blood pressure cuffs inflated time and again, and we spiked and dumped bag after bag of fluids into her veins. We escalated the medications, using more and more potent chemicals after it became clear that one had failed to resuscitate her: bolus, then dopamine, then bolus, then narcan, then bolus, then romazicon, then bolus, then norepinephrine, then bolus. Each drug targeted a different system, a different problem, a different potential root cause. None had a positive result. Fran was moaning in agony, breathing heavy and hard.

The little green lines that blip across on the cardiac monitor, the notorious EKG waves, tell me a lot about the heart and how it is—or often is not—functioning. After about fifteen minutes of all this hustle and chaos, we noticed a sudden change in Fran's heart rhythm. A brief glance at the lines running across the machine told me that she had suffered a major cardiac event with damage to large areas of her heart.

We called the attending physician to the room, and the family tearfully surrounded the bed. Fran was still fighting, but I was sure she would die within moments. The physician told the family that we could continue to invasively work on Fran by transferring her to the intensive care unit and inserting more lines and drains and tubes into her. The family cried. "No," they said, shaking their heads. "Just let her be. Let her go, let her go."

So we all took a step back. With one last run to the med room, this time for morphine, we stopped the IVs. We shut down the cardiac monitor, the lines, and the drips. No more blood pressure cuff. The room was quiet for the first time since she came into it.

But Fran kept breathing. In fact, she began to breath more easily as the right amount of morphine helped relax the diaphragm muscles and reduced the amount of work she had to do to take a breath. She was still obtunded and yellow, but at least she was comfortable.

When someone is actively dying, once all things have been tried, and if everyone is in agreement with the patient's wishes, we shift to providing palliative, or comfort care. It's like what hospice provides but in the hospital. Once again, I thought Fran had reached the end and expected her to pass away within minutes.

But Fran kept breathing on her own.

The amount of morphine we give for comfort care is never enough to actually make someone die, but sometimes—when we use it to help take away pain and help the body relax and not work so hard—we see the body shut down as a result of finally being able to rest. It was the end of my shift. Actually, it was past my shift. The night nurses had arrived, and I was responsible for briefing my replacement, the night charge nurse, about the status of the floor. I left, expecting to never see Fran again.

The next morning, while I was getting a floor-status report from the charge nurse I was relieving, I saw that Fran's room was not empty. She was still there, still alive. She continued to live when I finished my last shift that week. We did everything we could to make her comfortable, to ease the effort of her breathing, but for some reason Fran was still not ready to go. Clinically speaking, given her age and condition, I was amazed that she was still alive. The family just laughed wryly. "Well, Fran had always been spunky. A fighter. An independent woman." When I returned several days later, she was gone. Thrown back into a new set of thirty-two urgent stories, I never found out how, when, or if Fran died. I am pretty sure she did (or will, in her time), but I never found out how her story ended.

No one knows the day or hour when death will come for them. We calculate our odds and try to ensure ourselves against checking out too early or lingering too long. I see those who have tried to hasten the day through suicide. I see those who will grasp at anything, no matter how invasive or expensive, to buy a few more days.

The human body is fearfully and wonderfully made. It is not a fragile, hot-house flower that wilts easily. We are tougher than we realize, and harder to kill. It takes a prodigious effort to kill ourselves with drink, drugs, food, or tobacco—the real tragedy of self-abuse is not that it is casual but determined. And when our organs begin to shut down, as Fran's liver did, other systems in our body often compensate, adjusting to maintain homeostasis, fighting to keep the fire from going out. But at the same time, we often underestimate our own fragility.

Sometimes, death catches us off guard. "Jan," I said calmly into the phone, "I think you better get back up here. I just don't like the way your dad is looking." Within two hours he was dead. A few subtle changes in his blood pressure and mental status, over the course of an hour first thing in the morning, had given me a feeling. Call it nurses' intuition or whatever, but there are times when I know something is not right inside a patient's body. I can't always put my finger on it, but every nurse knows hypersensitive urgency, when a gut feeling deep inside starts screaming at you that something is wrong, even before labs or tests indicate what it is. I was glad that I called her.

I called one of my favorite doctors, and he listened as I hesitantly tried to describe my hunch. "I know you were just up here to see him, but his pressure is slightly lower and there is a definite change in mental status. I don't know, but something just isn't right." Even just in the short time I have been a nurse (some co-workers have been at this longer than I have been alive), I have learned to respect and value the all the physicians at our hospital, but there are a few who I come to trust more deeply. Usually, it's because I have worked beside them through some intense cases and respected the way they treated the patient and the nurses. They answered my questions, and I came to value the wisdom of their judgment.

He came up, and he agreed with me that the man had taken a turn for the worse. He talked to the family at length about treatment options, and the doctor decided to give the patient all the antibiotics and fluids that we could and watch to see how he would react. I would never have predicted how rapidly the situation would change. Before he was admitted late last night, which was not his first admission, he was healthy and functioning reasonably well. I tucked him, turned him, and checked him over just as the family arrived that morning and finished their discussion with the physician. I left the room, intending to make a few phone calls. Five minutes later, the daughter walked out of his room calmly and said, "Abby, I think dad is gone."

He had passed swiftly but peacefully. Smiling through her tears, she said, "He was happy. He lived a good life. It was just his time." With his family surrounding him, disease progressing through his body, he calmly let go. I can usually smell death a mile away, but this time, even though I knew that something was not right, he surprised me. Even with all of our advanced technology, we can't predict what the human body and spirit will do.

It is one thing to watch a stranger die, and quite another to sit with someone you love while they die. Richard Anderson was my grandpa. I could fill a whole book with stories about him, but I think the thing I loved most about him was this funny whistle that followed him everywhere. I grew up hearing that whistle while he putzed down by his boat, or put logs in his wood-stove, or strategized his next play in a game of cards. It was a low, breathy, random melody that slipped out subconsciously as his hands and body kept moving. He made music without giving it any more thought than breathing. It was always there, when he was focused, when he was stressed, when he was happy, when he was tired. Breathe in oxygen, exhale music. He was like that all the time. And his steady song was like a rock in our family. He was steady. In the face of birth and death and change and laughter and fear, he steadied us all. Never changing. Breathing in what was there around him and breathing out truth and hope and wisdom.

When my grandpa breathed his last, I was reading a psalm to him. I exchanged the last bit of oxygen and carbon dioxide with him. We knew he was going to die. With the help of hospice we had set up a scheduled vigil with family at his bedside twenty-four hours around the clock. It was my night with him. My Grandma slept bedside him in the bed, exhausted from long days of waiting for the inevitable, while I sat watch with grandpa. I perched on a chair borrowed from the dining room, facing him while he lay sunken deep into the pile of pillows layered on the hospital bed, both of us waiting for death, but neither of us knowing when he would arrive. Neither one of us sleeping, but neither one of us really awake. Hours into the middle of the night, breathing together, each breath precious, each one labored. As I read his favorite psalm, my hushed words fell lightly between the cracks of his raspy, rhythmic, labored exchange. Simultaneously exchanging carbon dioxide and oxygen, facing each other, the only sound in the dark room was our breathing, back and forth, between his gasps and the faltering rise and fall of my own chest. Each time he would breathe in, I would breathe out a sigh of relief. One more life-sustaining switch of chemicals and ions, one more effective exchange of ventilation and oxygenation. No whistle came out now, but the peace that he exuded with each breath sang a song louder than any he had ever whistled before.

Watching my grandpa die was the most sacred moment I have experienced. Death filled the air around his debilitated body, palpable in the air, but as he sucked in huge mouthfuls of it with every rise and fall of his chest, he belted out a song of hope, a holy exaltation of praise. Death for him held no fear. Breathe in the end of one life, only to breathe out into the new beginning of another. The hope his breath released took away my fear. I sat in this sacred exchange, in hopeful awe, strangely joyful, watching him die, sucking in the peace and hope he let out with his breath. Closing my eyes, I could hear his whistle in my heart. His steady whistle-song of confidence and faith, still coming in and out with every breath he took. My warm hand, still pink and pulsating, wrapped around his stiff white fingers; his cold, almost lifeless body giving life to my warm, fully-functioning frame. His labored breath taking in my fear and exchanging it, changing it, into a song of hope. His breathy song exchanging the death and despair that hung in the room, turning it into a loud exhalation of joy and praise. Strange, but in hearing his last breath, I have this eerie feeling that it sounded much like his first. Full of hope of what was next, full of the mystery and promise of part of his story that was not yet told. In his last breath in this life, I heard his first breath in the next. In his last breath, he reminded me that he had reason to hope.

I don't know everything. There are many people who have watched more deaths than I could count. People who have watched spouses and children and lifelong friends die. Many people have experienced death in ways I do not know. But I do know there is a relationship created by two people when both exchange oxygen and carbon dioxide together, while one slowly begins to breathe their last. Both are changed by that exchange. As a nurse, my charge is to breathe in death and fear and despair and breathe out hope and healing and peace in a rhythmic cycle of back and forth, in and out. I offer my dying, naked patient hope for what is next, peace and presence while they wait, but the reverse is also true. They offer me hope as they meet death face to face, breathing him in while not letting go of what is true. Hands on dying naked bodies, I am honored to be part of that sacred exchange, because in it I am changed. In it, I learn how to breathe in death and breathe out hope.

Doctors and nurses are experts in death, of course. Like mechanics who can predict failure by the hums, rattles, and clanking of an engine, educated guesses are fairly accurate. But we are not always right because people are not machines. God breathed life into the dust of the earth. That flame keeps its own schedule, known only to the One who lit it. At once fragile and fleeting, other times resilient, like a weed pushing its way through cracked concrete. Psalm 90:12 is a prayer for wisdom. It asks God to focus our minds on the time we have left as the means to living well: "Teach us to number our days aright, that we might gain a heart of wisdom." That number is known only to God, but as we draw nearer to him we realize how small it is. That is the heart of wisdom.

I find myself whistling at work now. Subconsciously, hands busy drawing blood, cleaning up stool, washing a bloody wound. It's a low, breathy song that has started bubbling up and out of me. Breathing in death all around me and breathing out a quiet song of hope; breathing out a hope-filled whistle song of my own.

Eight

Family

It took me some time to write this book—long enough that, during the course of the project, I met a man, dated, fell in love, got engaged, planned a wedding, and got married. My life changed enough that I'm not the same person that wrote the earliest pages of the manuscript (no, I won't tell you which ones those are).

Our wedding was on a hot, summer evening, just a few miles from the hospital. Every bride thinks her wedding is wonderful, and I'm no exception. Both of our dads are pastors, and so the father of the bride and father of the groom tag-teamed officiating the ceremony. It was a celebration of family and faith and a pledge of fidelity forever. Everyone in the wedding party and all the guests looked amazing. The room was great and the food was fun. We were young and fit as we stepped forward to face the future with twinkles and tears of joy filling our eyes.

Neither of us had any hesitation in our heart as we pledged to follow this wherever it led, for better or for worse.

I thought I understood what family meant to some of my patients before my marriage, but it was only intellectual knowledge. Only through my own marriage have I begun to grasp that a spouse is like a limb or vital organ. When one spouse's condition or care necessitates separation from their other half, we are dividing a symbiotic being. A patient's condition is not merely their own condition, it is the couple's condition. Those of us who presume to heal must factor that into our treatment, or we fail to care for the whole person.

The gastrointestinal physician told him he was a "special case." In and out of the hospital over the last several months, I recognized him as soon as I walked into the room. Defying all predictions, his intestinal tract was unresponsive to every known treatment. No matter what procedures were attempted, he kept bleeding, so he kept coming back in to see me.

Actually, I should say, "they," because his wife never left his side. Over the last several months, she had spent more time driving him to different appointments and to and from the hospital than doing anything else. Fifty-eight years of marriage, and the only nights they had spent apart were the ones he spent with us, at the hospital. He towered over her five foot frame, but she made up for it with spunk and strength. She was a commanding presence by his bedside, talking with doctors and taking notes. But the unending stress had more of a deep psychological impact on her than either of them realized. One morning, after their breakfast served on hospital trays, they attempted a walk to the family waiting room for some coffee. He in his hospital gown with IV bags hanging overhead, she gripping his hand with encouragement. I don't know who was more surprised when she suddenly grabbed her chest and sank to the floor. A huge commotion broke out as he tried to catch her, and bystanders started yelling for help. Now totally unconscious of his own health concerns, he was more tearful than she was as I wheeled her off to the emergency room.

A few hours later, she was an inpatient in the room right next to his; she was tired and tearful but stable. Doctors ran all sorts of tests on her heart and brain to make sure they ruled out every big, scary pathophysiology that can cause a sudden syncopal episode. But, in the end, the physicians decided that the stress of caring for, worrying about, and advocating for her husband had manifested itself physically in her frail body. Her heart was so deeply connected to his that disease and pain in his physical body affected hers.

The next morning, I saw them both in hospital gowns, sporting a matching set of IV poles, sipping coffee out of white Styrofoam cups. As I checked their matching blood pressures, I could not help but to recall the phrase, "In sickness or in health, for better or worse, until death do us part."

The family tree is a familiar metaphor but not rich enough to describe the wonder of our lives together. I imagine two saplings poking up through the soil a few yards apart. Not far, from our perspective, but almost impossibly distant to the pencil-sized plants. Surely they don't know of each other's existence. But as they reach for the sun, the forces of the forest—patches of light, density of soil, prevailing winds—push them together. Six or eight feet tall, their upper branches touch, find welcome, and become entangled like two young people courting. Still, they grow, but now their trunks, which seemed so far apart when they were young, bump and slide against each other, each twisting around the other's contours. Eventually, they become entwined, branch to root, so the passerby cannot easily distinguish where one begins and the other ends. They become a single, symbiotic life. In time, they drop their seeds around them, and the next generation sprouts. Underground, a vast root system unites all these lives in deep, inseparable community. The forest is a family.

As a nurse, I am constantly reminded that even withered old trees, bare of leaves, have deep tap roots, anchoring them into this community. Sometimes that's all they have left.

Several weeks later, I was knuckle-punched in the face. The punch was planted out of the blue as I leaned over, trying to calm her loud, frantic screams. She had been with us for a week, so our hallway resonated with sporadic bursts of screaming outrage, disturbing patients, families, and visitors for seven long days. We couldn't get her to eat, or to take pills, or to turn in bed. We were all at our wits' end. Her end-stage dementia affected her perception of everything around her, as well as her ability to communicate, so when she was upset, the only thing she could do was scream. Loudly. Which got us all running and hovering and trying to figure out what the problem was. Pain? Incontinence? Fear? It was a guessing game, one that I apparently lost. I was attempting to communicate therapeutically, responding to her screams with quiet, calming words, using whatever clinical assessment skills I could think of to guess the underlying problem that was upsetting her.

Her punch told me that I had guessed wrong. I asked if she needed more blankets, and I didn't even see it coming as I leaned in close to try and interpret her response. She scrunched up her wrinkled face, opened her toothless mouth, and popped her fist, fast as lightening, right into my nose. I didn't quite know what to do—get mad or laugh?—at getting punched in the face by a crazed, ninety-year-old woman. I turned and walked out into the hallway, holding my face in my hands, and let out a deep sigh, mentally preparing myself for the next bout of screams, knowing that she probably wouldn't even recognize the face she just punched.

But it was strangely silent for the next hour. Tentatively, I poked my head into her room to make sure she was still breathing. Not only was she alive, but she was sitting up and eating a snack while her daughter chatted away as if she didn't have a care in the world. The fist-slugger of a patient was a different woman. She came alive with her family there. Their voices, their touch, their faces, triggered something normal in her. Even though she couldn't tell me what her own name was, she somehow knew deep down inside that she was surrounded by family. By love. By hope-filled hearts. And she responded. For the first time since I had met her, she was quiet and peaceful. In fact, I hardly recognized her.

Her family didn't seem to mind the drool, the screams and mumbles, or the stiffly contracted arms and legs. They loved and served her without hesitation. Hair got curled and fluffed, nails were painted, family gossip was discussed, normal conversation and laughter filled the room. They saw her for who she was inside, not the crazed woman we encountered. They loved her. And their love changed her. Healed her. The safety of their circle centered her. Held her. Reoriented her to what was true, what she knew of life. Even though her brain was completely gone, her heart knew her own family.

I like to imagine what it will be like to grow old with my husband. I want us to catch glimpses of each other's wrinkled faces and remember how we looked on our wedding day. My work, however, is a daily reminder that love gives us those dreams, but life makes no such promises. I have seen too many stung by lack of recognition in a patient's eyes. We accept that the years weaken our bodies, but it seems too cruel for them to steal our memories.

Adult diapers hung out the back of his disheveled gown as he shuffled his tenth lap around the nurses' station. His hair was fuzzed and matted on his head as it swayed and bobbled mindlessly while he paced. His wife leaned over to kiss him anyway, undisturbed by his appearance. Hand-in-hand, they walked around and around to keep him from getting agitated, she chatting away as if he could still hear and comprehend words and conversation. Occasionally, one or two of his words in response were understandable, but most of the flow from his lips was mumbled gibberish that no one could interpret. It didn't phase her. She looked up at him as if he was still every ounce of the man she had married sixty years prior.

While she spoon-fed him yogurt that he dribbled down his chin, she wiped his spills and told me how his disease had progressed. A diagnosis of Alzheimer's two years ago had been devastating, but he had remained stable, and she had managed to be able to care him for him at home until the month prior to his admission. He began wandering into the street and explosively throwing furniture. Those and other erratic, unsafe behaviors were too much for her to handle on her own. They spent a month in and out of different nursing homes, but none would take him. And so, with no place else to go, they ended up at the hospital.

I only saw her cry once. She was talking about how hard it was for her to watch his frustration and confusion progress. Her heart ached to watch him struggle. But she kept on loving him as the husband she always knew him to be, just as the wife she always had been. In his condition, his behavior was unpredictable. One minute he would be fine, resting normally, and the next he could be up, agitated and yelling. Patiently, she studied what triggered his reactions and did everything she could to create an environment that would help reorient and calm him when he got frustrated. Watching, studying, nurturing, hovering —she knew his moods and his needs without him needing to say a word. He really couldn't, anyway. She kept on loving, even when his mind stopped recognizing the love of his life. She kept on loving, even when he shook her hand off his shoulder and paced in circles, confused and not wanting help or comfort from the woman who committed her life and all to him.

He stayed a week or two with us, while the social workers and case managers met with her to try to find a place that would care for him adequately. Packed and loaded in a wheelchair, she pushed him out to the car, all the while talking all about their new adventure and the things they would do together. Hand on his back, she gave him all the dignity and honor she could muster, completely committed to him no matter what would come next.

Will my husband forget me in a cloud of dementia, or I him? I hope not. But in the end, we are not trees or beasts. We are men and women, gifted by our Creator with the ability to choose love and loyalty. Our vows are not given for the good times—who needs a promise that someone will enjoy you at your best? We exchange vows to know that someone has our back when life does its worst.

I have a front row seat to the gladiatorial pit of human existence. I have seen cruel abandonment, men and women left to face their darkest hour without a loved one by their side. But I have also seen spouses and siblings, parents and children, rise and perform acts of love so holy and heroic that I am humbled. Because of that, I dare to hope that my husband and I will really be able to love each other as Christ loves us.

Nine

Present

Like most of us humans born into the world, I have an innate desire to make a difference in the world. But what my patients consistently show me is that often the biggest change happens in the smallest moments. Moments that come not because of heroic acts, but in learning to see people for who they really are, in asking simple questions and sometimes, in simply being present.

I didn't do anything to help her. In fact, I was on duty for only four hours of her stay, and she actually got worse under my care. I knew her diagnosis and was quite sure of her prognosis, but I was helpless do anything to improve it. An aggressively spreading cancer that necessitated invasive surgery while she grew weaker by the moment meant slender odds for a full recovery. I think that she and her husband understood this, but they didn't appear paralyzed or driven by fear of the unknown like some.

Stoic wasn't the right word— maybe *resolved* would be more accurate.

The physician came by and asked her if, all things considered, she still wanted to proceed with the surgery scheduled for the next morning. The doctor was honest about how desperate the surgery was. It held only the possibility of improvement, not a promise. It wouldn't cure her, but it was her only fighting chance. I could tell by the look on her face that she was not feeling good. No medication I gave her seemed to be enough to ease her constant pain and unshakeable nausea. She nodded her head through the waves of dry heaving and said without hesitation, "Let's do it. Let's get it over with."

Sometimes all I can do is to be a kind presence alongside people during the worst moments of their lives. In her case, even if I was the world's best nurse (which I most definitely am not), she, her husband, and I all knew I couldn't make her better. Of course, my first thought and every instinct is to *do something,* to take on their disease and proactively fight with every weapon in our considerable modern arsenal. But when my technical quiver is out of arrows, I am at first anxious. And then I remember at those moments, I can at least be there with them. When there are no fixes, answers, therapy, medicines, when I have nothing tangible to give, I can give that. I can sit there in silence while the doctor speaks, after he leaves, and as they wait for the gurney to come take them to surgery.

And so I sat there next to her bed, just sitting next to her. There was nothing else I could do, but I could do that. And she was okay with that. It seemed to be enough, to give her and her husband hope that they could face the unknown because they were not alone.

Last week I wanted to be left alone. I'd had enough. I had been spit on, screamed at, cussed out, punched out, pooped on, and chased out. I didn't want to be present for anyone or have anyone present with me. Stick a fork in me, I was done.

But one morning near the end of this very terrible week, a man barged in on my conversation with the previous shift's charge nurse. It was early, and I had just arrived. I hadn't had my coffee and was barely awake. I wanted to get my report finished on what had happened through the night, and ease into my day.

He lit into me. "You are all incompetent! Why don't you learn to do your job? I am tired of stupid nurses in here not knowing what is going on!"

I didn't even have time enough to open my mouth to say good morning or introduce myself before he was screaming, inches away, waving his fist in my face. With his red, sweaty forehead towering over me, his voice found another gear. "I demand to know what is going on! If I have to deal one more minute with this shit, I am going to do something about it!" He was shaking with rage, blowing up at me. I took in his bulging, bloodshot eyes, his pulsating jugular vein, and his spittle-glazed lips as he formed his words with exaggerated, dramatic movement. He was out of control, and I had no idea who he was or what he was so pissed off about. I hadn't seen him on my last shift.

I tried but couldn't get a word in edgewise. Now I was pissed off. I didn't know what his problem was, but whatever it was, it wasn't my fault. How dare he attack me?

As I listened, I gathered that his wife had come in during the night, and he was obviously unhappy with the care she was receiving. As he ranted, my mind formed a nasty rebuttal. He didn't like the nurses? Well, as far as I was concerned, he had plenty of other hospitals to choose to go visit.

I was just about to cut loose with my own tirade when something inside of me told me to pause. I ignored his screaming and listened to what he was saying: "I have been here all night, and no one has told me a thing! Why can't any one of you idiots tell me what is wrong with my wife?!?"

I heard and saw something. I don't know if it was the way his voice quaked when he said, "My wife," or if it was the dark circles under his eyes, sinking into his cheeks. I was tired, but he looked exhausted. The scene froze for a moment as he paused, and I held my fire.

In my mind, I peeled back the layers of his rage. I looked past his open mouth, which now looked more desperate than snarling. Underneath the anger and insults, I saw his heart nakedly exposed for a moment. This tirade had nothing to do with me, and while his fury was directed at the staff, it wasn't about them, either. As I looked into his bloodshot eyes, I saw fear.

He was in love with his wife. And he was terrified that he was going to lose her. He was staring into the abyss.

All of my defensiveness evaporated. I regrouped and told myself, "Breathe, Abby. You are not really seeing him." I sat down and extended my hand in greeting. He stared but let it hang there as I spoke.

Abby Jackson

"Sir, my name is Abby. I am going to be your wife's nurse today. I am going to do everything I possibly can to get her better. Let's talk about how I can help right now." And I sat there, hand out, waiting for a response. Stiffly, almost mechanically, he shook it. But at that moment, armistice was declared. The battle was over; everything had changed.

"I just don't understand," he said. "I was so careful at home, taking care of her. I followed all the doctor's instructions. I can't believe she got this sick." His posture, only moments ago poised for attack, slumped. His shoulders started shaking. His bloodshot eyes now pleaded with me, wanting someone to help, to stand beside him on the edge of that abyss.

A few minutes later, I left his wife's room, full of adrenaline but still a bit shaken, and called a few physicians. A few minutes after that, I went back in and told him what I'd learned from them. For the rest of that shift, someone would have thought that he and I were best friends. I didn't do anything for him or his wife that day that was especially caring or clever. I wasn't a heroic healer or miracle worker.

But I was there with him, really present, through one of the worst days of his life. And that mattered.

Several weeks later, I was in charge and was just moving through my normal routine when I unexpectedly found myself crying on the phone. I was just trying to help another busy nurse by making a call about one of her patients. I ended up talking to a woman by accident and was blindsided by the encounter.

A male patient had come in late in the night and needed surgery urgently. There wasn't much time to get things organized. The surgeon had come around early in the morning and decided to schedule the OR immediately, but because of how sick the patient was and his history of mild dementia, the doctor wanted to consult with the patient's family before proceeding with the operation. I was the charge nurse that day, so I volunteered to make some calls.

I called every number we had trying to track someone down. We didn't have much information on this patient, other than that he had been sent over during the night from a nursing home. Someone said that he lived there with his wife, who reportedly also had severe health problems. I left voicemails for a couple of distant family members, but we were hoping to connect with someone more immediate. It was still early, and the administrative staff at the nursing home weren't in yet. I found a number that I thought might connect me to the on duty nurse there. When I dialed, I assumed I would get someone who who could give me clinical information and track down family contacts.

A thick, muffled voice answered with a very labored, "Hello?" It took several minutes of awkward conversation to deduce that I had accidentally reached his wife, who I figured out was struggling with severe expressive aphasia related to a stroke. Communication was difficult.

My first instinct was to apologize and ask her to let me talk to the staff in order to get the information I needed. But when I explained that I was a nurse and that I was calling about her husband, the tone in her voice stopped me.

She was so excited to hear his name. "How is he?" she asked arduously. "How is my sweetheart?"

I could barely understand her and had to have her repeat everything she said at least once. Her tongue was thick, and it made her voice sound childish. It was an effort for her to form her words, and she struggled to stutter in an attempt to express herself.

I gave her an abbreviated version of his condition, and one would have thought I just handed her a million bucks.

"I did... not know," she mumbled. "I did... not know. How he... was. Can you. Can you tell... my sweetheart... I love him? Please, tell him I love him!"

She had been up all night since they had taken him away, wondering and worrying with no way of finding out if the love of her life was hurting or alone, or even alive.

"Thank you! Oh, thank... you!" Over and over she repeated her gratitude for hearing his name and learning of his condition, for discovering what had happened to him. And then came the question that took me completely off guard and filled my eyes with tears.

"Thank you so much! Thank you. What is your name? Do you have gooheed in your heart? Do you love him?"

It took several attempts at getting her to speak more clearly into the phone before I figured out that she was asking me, "Do you have God in your heart?" She asked me again, and I stopped. Here was this woman, severely debilitated, alone, unable to even be with her husband of sixty-plus years while he went through desperate surgery, and she wanted to know about *me*. She cared enough to ask who I was, and about my heart, if I was someone who loved God. Because she was sure that God loved me. She wanted to know if I knew it.

A stranger that I have never and will never meet—at least on this earth in this life—was trying to penetrate my professional layers. In my work, those layers protect us from being hurt. It's dangerous to expose your heart nakedly. And so we focus on our responsibilities, on skills and tasks and numbers. But these defenses can keep us from being present for others and from others being present for us.

"Yes," I answered after a moment of silence, "Yes, I do love God. He is in me, in my heart."

I could hear the excitement in her broken voice as if she had just made a new best friend, "Oh, I will pray for you!" I was humbled. My stress faded as I held the phone close to my ear, wanting to let this moment last a little longer. She should have been the anxious one, but instead, she was the one offering me hope and peace, gratitude, and compassion. She was present for me.

I had a hard time hanging up the phone. I wanted to preserve that feeling, that this woman who could not do anything for me cared and wanted to know me. I wanted to learn from her how to be better at being there for others. Sometimes that's all we can give, but sometimes it's all the other person needs.

Ten

Change

Crazy hair sprung out in all directions as she peered through a hole in the mound of sheets she had pulled over her head. Certifiably insane, she had as many personalities as she had diagnoses. Bloodshot bug eyes tossed daggers at anyone entering the room. "Don't touch me!" she screamed as I put my stethoscope to her lungs. No one had been able to go near her or give her food or medication for hours. She insisted that we were all trying to kill her.

I kept coming back, hoping that one of her many personalities might be willing to work with me. After several more hours and multiple attempts, she slowly pulled the sheets off her face, and eyed me skeptically as I putzed around the room, chatting about life and weather, gradually making my way closer to her fort on the bed. Eventually, I claimed a corner of the bed and just sat and talked. She just glared back, stubborn and silent.

As I got up to leave again, she begrudgingly shrugged and asked, "Well, aren't you going to change me?"

Captive to whichever of her personalities refused to let anyone know (although we all did), she had been laying in her own urine, unable to clean herself. Now someone in there was willing to ask for help. I was afraid to appear too eager or aggressive and break the moment, so I casually replied, "Well, absolutely I will." And we moved forward. She let me wash her, warm soapy water on her back and all the way down to her toes. I am not sure when the last time was that she had access to clean water or clean clothes. Her adult foster care home had been destroyed in a fire, and she had been bouncing from church cots to random couches. Tragedy followed her even more persistently than her mental illness. She never talked about it, but our social worker shared how this patient's sister had just died and explained how no family was available to take her to the funeral. The conversation we had during her bath consisted of me chatting away and her glaring at me in cold silence while I rubbed her back and attempted to tame her wild hair. She will never remember me or the conversations we had or the dignity I tried to offer her, but I know that at least for that morning, she was treated like a real woman with worth and value. I didn't fix her or solve her problems, but the most healing thing I could offer was to clean her dirty body. And five minutes later, another angry personality popped to the surface and the connection we had vaporized. Later that day, I packed her up in a wheelchair and sent her off by ambulance to her sister's funeral. Alone. I watched her crazy hair hang low as she was wheeled out the door. Despite anything I did, she left just as crazy and broken and lost as when she came in.

Several weeks prior, I had another patient who left hating my guts. She suffered from chronic pain and kept showing up at different emergency rooms around the city in an attempt to get relief through narcotics.

She was young, almost my age, and had lived through countless tragedies. Deaths and abuse and poverty exacerbated her mental and physical addiction to substances. I tried for several days to compassionately, yet firmly, set boundaries and find a way to help figure out the root of her sometimes legitimate health concerns. By the end of the third day, she was screaming at me for pain medications that she thought she needed. I patiently and lovingly tried to explain our plan of care and ask her for permission to work together to figure out the best solution for her. We paged physicians and got a special pain management team on board for her care, but she was livid. And she screamed in my face when she didn't get what she wanted. She stormed out the door, angry and unwilling to hear my genuine care and compassion for her story. My work with her had changed nothing.

These stories are common at this hospital. Our Catholic tradition and strategic location in the heart of our inner city are intentionally oriented toward advocating for the down-and-out, the abused and abusive, the underserved and underprivileged, the homeless and addicted, the lonely and confused, those sick in the heart as well as body. We have a mercy fund that helps cover expenses for those who fall between government assistance and insurance red-tape, so we treat them all, regardless of income or finances. We welcome patients who live through disease alone without any insurance or well-intended advocates.

But despite our good intentions and works, this work can feel futile. I often walk away from my day discouraged and struggling to find any hope at all. I see death and disease covering everything I touch. There are days I make a difference in fending them off, and there are days when the inevitable is much larger than the fight I put up. It gets old. I want patients to actually get better, to wake up with clear minds and normal bodies. But I am learning that healing and hope sometimes looks different than I imagined.

I started going to counseling after I became a nurse. I started my job, took on the world, and promptly became depressed about it all. The heaviness and darkness in the world overwhelmed me. A year or so into my career, I took a trip to sub-saharan Africa, and it probably put me over the edge. Months of seeing poverty and starvation and inhuman living conditions there deepened my depression and made me angry. I struggled daily after I came back from that trip and confronted the mystery of unanswered prayer in the stories of patients who never got better— sometimes because their problems were too big or their desire to change too small. My counseling sessions only drove me deeper into a wrestling match with God. I was trying to trust in the goodness of God when I couldn't make sense of His ways.

Part of my struggle was coming to see that it isn't about me. I wanted to be a healer of hurts and a solver of problems. It is freeing to eventually realize—which I did through my counseling—that I am not the solution to humanity's brokenness. God answered my questions with some serious questions of His own, like, "Who is this who questions my wisdom with such ignorance?" And I had to answer Him back honestly, "It is I—and I was talking about things I knew nothing about, things far too wonderful for me. I had only heard about you before, but now I have seen You with my eyes... I know that You can do anything, and no one can stop You" (Job 42:2-5). There is a mystery to how God works and why He does what He does that I will never understand, but I know that my part is to trust that in every heart, in every broken body, in every dark story, He sees value. He is enough to offer hope and healing.

Last week, when I found myself dodging poop-filled towels and angry fists for the third time that morning from a patient I was trying to help, it only reinforced the "why" I ask myself on a regular basis. I don't do this because I want to "help people." I can't help most of them. And I don't do this because "I want to make a difference;" because in the end, it won't matter how nice or compassionate I was. It will never be enough. All my good efforts will fade away. The truth is that no amount of do-gooding on my part can take away the pain and suffering that many of my patients go through on a regular basis. I don't keep going back because I think I can make a difference; I keep going back because they are worth it. As men and women created in God's image, they are worth my effort. I keep going back because each naked, angry, ugly, old body is worth it. Each one is sacred, and they deserve to be treated that way. I learned to endure needles and blood and guts because each life, no matter how young or old, rich or poor, brilliant or dumb, nice or evil, is worth the dignity of my respect. I imagine myself in that gown, naked and exposed. I want to do unto them as I would have others do unto me.

In doing so, I stand with generations of nuns who have carried the mantle of compassion and never gave up. They knew that regardless of death and disease, every life was worth the effort. That's what Christ taught us.

I remember seeing this figure perched on Grandma's fireplace hearth when I was six and peering with obsessive curiosity at the mysterious object. In my mind, I can still see her staring down at me while I write this paragraph. Her eyes are pale blue, her cap shiny white, and her crisp uniform has a pale red cross at the neck. I have known her all my life. She was a gift given to my Grandma to celebrate her becoming a nurse. Whenever Grandma would tell stories about her nursing adventures in exotic places, her eyes would wander up to the figurine. I would stare at that little nurse until I was convinced that I could see the Himalayan jungles and smoky thatch huts in her glass eyes and smell the spicy curry and incense soaked into her glass uniform. She never left my Grandma's mantle, a constant reminder of her stories and adventures around the world. Every time I would visit and sit with scones and coffee on the couch, we would stare each other down. She was a magical object, a doorway to a wonderful and heroic world, like the wardrobe in the Chronicles of Narnia. Sometimes, Grandma would look at her and be reminded of another story. The best ones were told again and again and again. As a kid, I ate them up. They were food for my soul, which was hungry for heroes. I learned and memorized all her stories: late night escapades, dodging tigers in the jungle just in time to birth a baby in a hut; nursing hundreds back to health with nothing but her nursing books and a lot of gumption; her healing hands on the sweaty dying brows of patients with typhoid and leprosy; tales of heart-ache and loneliness and perseverance, all suffered to bring hope and healing. There was no question in my mind that I must become a nurse when I grew up, just like Grandma. When all else around me was dirty and chaotic, I would remain clean and calm and always put together, just like that glass figurine on the mantle.

When I was in nursing school and in my first months on the job, I would visit Grandma and the little glass nurse on my days off and cry over cups of her favorite coffee and hazelnut creamer. I was letting them both down; I felt like a mess, a pile of mistakes crumpled there at her pristine, white, glass feet. Grandma would set her coffee cup down, lick a finger to page through her weathered Bible, push her thick-rimmed glasses higher on the bridge of her nose, and start to pray. I would close my eyes and the room would fill. Fill with voices louder and bigger than hers or mine or the glass nurse. When Grandma prayed, I am convinced her voice thundered in the heavens, backed by a heavenly host of angels.

Since I became a nurse, my fearless, spunky Grandma has lost her husband, her bowels, and parts of her memory. I think of her and I picture that glass nurse staring down at me as I head into the hospital early in the morning and drive home late at night; just trying to live up to their standards.

Eleven

Porcelain

Up and down. Up and down. She was screaming in pain. In and out of the bed, she could not get comfortable, and nothing I could do was helping. More pillows. Too many pillows. Heating pad. Too hot. Pills. More pills. More pills. Different physicians with different ideas for different procedures waltzed in and out of the room but none with solutions. My knees on the bed behind her, my hands holding her shoulders, I tried to hold her together as she shook in pain and panic. Chronic pain had plagued her for years. She had learned to push through it and could put up with much, but this was more than she had ever experienced. A hard fall resulting in complex spinal fractures and nerve damage had completely disrupted her independent life. She had been forced into a new life without freedom as she knew it. There was no end in sight as the paralyzing pain dominated her days.

Abby Jackson

The nurse's call light was coming on every five minutes as she pushed the button to summon staff for desperate bathroom breaks and repositioning in the bed, all in futile attempts to find comfort. She looked at me with fear through a drugged stupor and whispered, "I just don't know what to do with myself." With crazy, scraggly hair she looked nothing like the dignified woman who traveled the world teaching nursing and lecturing hundreds about community health. She was a nurse herself, the worst kind of patient to have. She knew how things should be and tolerated nothing less than prompt efficiency. Forthright and sometimes shockingly blunt in her honesty, she said what she thought, all the time. She had always been passionate and spunky, not afraid to ask hard questions and demand concrete answers. Now there were no answers.

She was my Grandma.

This time I wasn't the nurse. This time it was my family. My love. My hero, my life's inspiration lay on the bed naked and in pain. And I learned a lot about being the family member on the other side of the call light. I see a lot in my job. I watch patients and families deal with disease and death on a daily basis. But now I have seen both sides of the system. I never thought I would see my strong nurse of a Grandma here, in the very hospital bed that she spent so many years of her life serving. As I watched her wrestle, I found myself remembering so many things that she had taught me, not only just about how to be a nurse, but how to struggle well. Here are a few things I have learned from my Grandma.

First, you will be there, sooner or later. Almost all of us will end up naked in a hospital. I will get sick. You will get sick. A spouse, a child, a parent, a friend will get sick. Life is fragile and short. Recently, I took care of an elderly gentleman who at eighty-two had never been admitted to the hospital before. But he couldn't avoid it forever. Our body's breakdown is inevitable. We break and tear and bruise and fail. Cancer, car accidents, infections, simple procedures gone wrong—all of these are beyond our power to control or foresee. The Old Testament Book of Ecclesiastes tells us that there is a healthy fear, a sacred awe that comes from choosing to remember just how fleeting life really is. Grandma talks about it everyday. "I may not be alive next time you see me," she reminds me bluntly. Struggles should not be a surprise to anyone; they will come in their time. What matters is how we respond. My dad would often quote one of his favorite sayings to us as kids when we were young: "Life is struggle. Either struggle poorly or struggle well. These are the options."

Both my grandparents constantly reminded me that life is sacred, so be grateful. Each day is a gift. The fact that your mind and eyesight are keen enough to read these words is something to be grateful for. A wizened old man I took care of recently smacked his dentures loudly with pleasure. "Suppertime!" It was his happy declaration, exploding with gusto from his eighty-five pound frame. He couldn't wait to dig into his pureed mystery meat slopped next to a pile of pureed corn. "MMM MMM MMM MMM MMMMM! Zhish ish schoo good!" he groaned loudly as every shoveled mouthful of pureed goodness dripped and sprayed all directions. I have never seen a man so incredibly excited about a meal. He giggled and shouted and moaned as if he was eating the greatest banquet ever spread before a man. I sat amazed. The mere smell of his dinner had sent my stomach into seizures of misery, but he was blissfully content. Because of several complex diagnoses, our care plan for him had changed his diet dramatically, so not only was he limited to only eating strictly pureed foods, he was also no longer allowed to feed himself. We had to spoon every bite into his mouth. A demoralizing situation for many of us to imagine for ourselves, but not for him. He was grateful for every bite, for the company and laughter at his jokes. For still being able to eat at all. I sat by his bedside table, helping him grasp the hospital silverware and scoop piles of messy pureed mush through his wiggly dentures. And I belly laughed as he made fun of himself and just delighted in the joy of a meal. He ate that mush with dignity. He had been a successful and well-known businessman in town, his career tied to famous people and exotic places in the world, and now he couldn't choose what or how he ate his dinner. But he was glad to be spoon-fed pulp by a young nurse.

I ran my first triathlon last year. It was terribly great. My roommate and I trained and trained and trained. All spring and summer, we ran on steamy, hot, humid days, and I swam lap after lap early mornings and late at night after long shifts at the hospital. I am not athletic, and I have never been a swimmer. But I was enticed by the challenge of trying something I had never done before. After several months, I could swim the required distance and got faster each week I practiced. My early mornings in the pool were calm and peaceful, with no one else there at 5:30 a.m. I got pretty good at swimming back and forth in that little box. But race day was a different story. The open water on Lake Michigan was choppy and windy with one to two foot crests. Freezing cold undertow surrounded by competitors wildly thrashing their limbs had not been part of my training. My quiet, little lap pool had not prepared me for this. I made it off the beach into the wild, open water of Lake Michigan and freaked out. I found myself in the midst of a race with a full-blown panic attack. I couldn't see the shore or the markers I was supposed to head towards. I wasn't tired, just overwhelmed by the feeling of being out of control. I seriously thought I was going to drown. Each stroke was a choice. I had to force myself to just keep moving. One arm up, deep breath, next arm, stroke, and again. I talked myself through each movement. After what seemed like forever, I finished the kilometer swim. It wasn't pretty, and I was the absolute last racer out of the water, but I finished. And the rest of the race was awesome.

I think that feeling of being completely out of control and in deep water is how we all feel when our bodies break or when the unexpected happens. I wasn't far from help but felt completely out of control. Some diseases are the consequence of our life choices, and some are a mystery. How, why, and when they develop can't be controlled, predicted, or prevented. A lot of things are going to happen that I cannot prepare for: disease, death, financial ruin, job loss, relationship struggles, accidents, natural disasters, wind, and waves. But I can choose how I will respond. My patient had learned that. He had every reason to be bitter and angry. He had lost his wife, his health, and his mind, but he didn't let it ruin him. His life was joy-filled because of how he chose to react to the things he couldn't control. His was a life that had always been infused with gratitude and joy, determined to see and remember the good. That served him well when the time came.

Grandma was never afraid to speak her mind. I have this crystal clear memory of being eleven years old and full of pre-teen sass when she sat me down and confronted me on my "issues with pride" and urged me to repent. She never let us settle for living in regret. She was unafraid of doing what it took to have relationships be right. Money and wealth are meaningless if you are alone when you get sick. I regularly see grown men who are deathly afraid of being sick and alone. One patient looked at me when I asked if I could help him call someone who would be a support for him while he waited for results from cardiac testing to determine if he needed major heart surgery. He replied that he hadn't yet taught his cat how to answer the phone (he was not joking). Estranged from his family, his brother had put him on hold when he called to tell him that the doctors thought he might be having a heart attack.

A while back, I had this patient at the hospital who was given a really dismal prognosis. There really was not much that the doctors could do for him, and when it came time for me to discharge him at the end of his stay, I sent him home with an understanding that he was just beginning a steady decline that would end in his death. He knew that.

All day long we had joked and talked a bit, but I was busy with other patients and did not have time to sit and process the situation with him. He kept making jokes about having me come take care of him at his house. I would just laugh and tell him he was being ridiculous. He was a big, tough, and gruff kind of guy. He seemed nonchalant, shrugging and making sarcastic comments while talking with the doctor. But as I walked him down to the front entrance of the hospital and sat with him while he waited for his taxi, he got real quiet. This man, who had not so much as batted an eyelash when the doctor told him he did not have long to live, looked at me as huge tears started rolling down his cheeks and said in a whisper I could barely decipher, "I am so afraid to die alone. I have no one." As I listened, I realized that I have never seen anyone as shaken by fear as he was in that moment. It was one of those moments when time seems to stop. All the chaotic movement around us, all the hustle and bustle of the hospital busyness faded to gray stillness, and I felt his raw fear, loneliness, and hopelessness. He would have given anything to turn back time and restore his broken relationships. Don't let relationships that matter decay and wither. Fight with all you have for restoration. Work through regret, don't run from it. Face it. Forgive and be forgiven.

Grace, give grace. Grandma gave it. And asked for it in return. We had a patient this last year who came in for some abdominal discomfort. X-rays showed serious problems with her bowels, and she was quickly rushed to the operating room. The unexpected surgery revealed a huge infection, and all the combined factors threw her eighty-four-year-old body into a hospital induced delirium. She hit and punched and spat and swore. Yelling at the nurses who were trying to help control her pain and do everything to help her body heal. Her family was mortified. She had never done anything like that before. We didn't know any different; all we knew was that she was wildly out of control. Our staff was challenged to respond to her violent lashing out and paranoid accusations with grace and compassion. A few days after her delirium cleared, she was leaving thank you notes for the staff and inviting us all to her birthday party. Pleasant and apologetic, she couldn't believe how she had acted. We all need grace at one time or another.

As I watched my Grandma bury the man she loved, sell her home, hear diagnosis after new diagnosis, lose her independence, and still have hope, I realized what she had been trying to teach me all along. I had dreamt my whole life of growing up to be just like that porcelain nurse–she and my Grandma, always amazingly courageous and perfectly compassionate. I thought that was what she wanted me to be too, pristine and always put-together. But as I watched her struggle, honest and naked, through loss and pain and death, I realized that the porcelain nurse didn't symbolize perfection, but fragility. Grandma knew her own porcelain fragility and because of that, she knew where to place her hope. She didn't rely on her own strength to be enough to save lives in India, raise a family, face death, and carry on, but her hope was in something bigger than herself. She faced (and still faces) her fragility and nakedness with hope.

My husband and I were buried in boxes. We had just gotten back from our honeymoon and were unpacking and opening wedding gifts. One of the last boxes I opened was wrapped round and round with bubble-wrap and packing peanuts. Digging through to the bottom of the box, my fingers brushed an all too familiar smooth, glassy surface. Staring up at me, with her perfect porcelain eyes, was the nurse. Grandma had passed on the porcelain nurse to me as a wedding present. As I gently swept the cellophane wrappings from her porcelain hands, I felt like I had finally discovered the secret she hid inside that glass heart. As I faced that little nurse, I felt like I was facing my own nakedness and fragility, and I realized I have a choice. A choice to put my hope in something (or someone) bigger than myself. Grandma had taught me so much about nursing, and people, and struggle, and grace, and prayer, but the true gift was buried deep in discovering beauty in my vulnerability.

Twelve

Prayer

I took my first breath in this place. It is wrapped through the strands of my DNA, mixed into my soul. My faith has its roots here, as my deeply Christian parents met and gave birth to me in this building. But the roots go deeper than that. In 1893, the Sisters of Mercy and Congregation of the Sisters of the Holy Cross started a fifteen bed hospital in a house they had acquired in downtown Grand Rapids. They were part of an order of women committed to serving the poor and bringing healing and hope to the oppressed. Although I am not Catholic and certainly no nun, their mission and ministry are as much a part of me as if I were.

Dawn may not be a nun with a life-long vow of celibacy, but the spirit of the living God is obvious within her. Her touch brings healing and hope. She lives the legacy of the sisters who founded this hospital. Her love is strong like ale, but bubbly like champagne. Her sassy heels and pink lipstick never stop her from getting down and dirty with those in need.

Dawn and I once spent several days with a patient who checked in only to be given a death sentence. Independent and healthy for a man in his late eighties, he and his family were shocked to learn that he had become so sick so fast. Hour after sad hour, bloody poop filled his bed, draining life and energy. Several times an hour we came to clean him, and every time, he thanked us and apologized for the trouble he thought he was putting us through (which he wasn't). As his body shut down, his dignity never missed a beat. He kept expressing his appreciation of our efforts (which was unnecessary) and graciously accepted our apologies: "We've done all we can" and "nothing more we can do."

Dawn and I spent hours with him and his family, hearing their stories and learning their inside jokes, watching them grieve and waiting for the inevitable. Each family does this in their own way, and every story ends a little differently. He had come in for some minor pain without realizing that he would never go out those doors alive. As death drew near, his family asked us for a favor: he wanted to see the sun one last time. He could accept that his story would end under florescent light, immersed in the sounds and smells of a hospital. But they wanted to give him just a few moments outside, in real sunlight.

It seemed like it should be a simple thing, but as we thought about how to pull it off, we realized that it wasn't. It was late fall in Michigan: cloudy, wet, cold, and windy. He was on intravenous drips and breathing high levels of oxygen through a mask. He could barely open his eyes, much less move. We were afraid that lifting him into a wheelchair might be too much for his weak state to handle. There was no easy way to position him to see the sun, either. We couldn't just wheel his bed through the lobby into the parking lot. I saw problems, but Dawn's grace and goodness are not easily intimidated. We pulled out a measuring tape. We began checking the width of equipment against doorways. We ran around the hospital property, scouting routes. We came up with a plan.

Assembling a team, we clustered and taped down equipment and found a way to move his entire hospital bed—oxygen tanks, monitors, IV drips, and all—through the hallways and elevators. We got him to a spot on the top floor where a set of doors led out to an area of the roof that had been converted to a "prayer labyrinth," a set of paths for walking and meditation. It took a lot of pushing and pulling, with plenty of bumping and rattling, to get the heavy mechanical bed and gear over door jambs and onto that roof.

As we jostled this contraption through the last set of service doors and onto the roof, I worried about the weather. None of us had seen the sun in days. There would be no next trip up here for this dying man. His window was now.

And then Christ took our water and made wine.

For perhaps minutes on that cold gray day, the sun shone warm and still. The patient lay there, quiet in his bed in the prayer path, propped up by piles of pillows. His family stood in a circle around him, holding hands. Hospital workers and others who came to use the prayer path stood back and stared. His oxygen tanks hissed, his drips ran, and sunlight bathed his face like God's own kiss.

His family had talked about faith, but as the sun shone on him, they were despondent. It was all tears and sniffles, with sadness hanging over the moment like a cloud. For those who don't fear death, it should have been a glorious and graceful moment, a time for joyful tears and final smiles. It could have been a last, glad, memorable goodbye for their patriarch. But his last time in the sun was turning heavy and foreboding. The silence was suffocating them.

Dawn and I stood outside their circle and watched. I thought, but she acted. She gently asked their permission to become part of the family for that moment.

Dying is an intimate thing. In our culture, that passage is usually witnessed only by spouses, the closest family members, or life-long companions. We are used to being there as professionals, but it's awkward and difficult to shed that role and step into that sacred moment. For the family, it is like inviting strangers into your closest family time.

But Dawn didn't hesitate. She stepped in, grabbed hands, touched the shoulders heavy-laden with grief, and started praying out loud for all to hear. I think all of heaven and earth stood still in that moment. I know for sure that everything and everyone on the fifth floor rooftop at the hospital fell still at the sound of her voice. Speaking into that silence, she offered a bold declaration of faith, a cry for love and healing, into that moment of mourning. Sunlight seemed to surround everyone with halos like rays of grace and mercy, and her voice resounded in the heavens. I felt hope.

"Our Father who art in heaven, hallowed be Your Name." As Dawn prayed the familiar words of the Lord's Prayer, I could almost hear the hundreds of nuns who had come before us in this place reciting the litany with her. She covered the family with comfort, her cadence carrying the rhythm of generations of faithful healers who had cried out these words on this spot.

"Your Kingdom come, Your will be done..." Her voice was confident and clear. She committed the lives of all of us who were there to the grace of a good God, trusting on behalf of those who didn't have the strength to trust, believing on behalf of those who didn't have the faith to believe, and asking on behalf of those who were too broken to ask for themselves.

"Give us this day our daily bread..." She asked the God of our fathers to bring them sustenance in the midst of their loss, the daily provision of hope, the bread of life, and satiation for longing hearts.

"Deliver us from evil..." Dawn was a "just" a nurse, but in that moment, she was standing up for the most vulnerable, those in mourning, those on their deathbed, calling down the angels in heaven to cover and protect them.

"For Yours is the Kingdom, and the Power, and the Glory, Forever. Amen." She pledged our finite existence to the power of a mysterious Eternal Being. I remember, at that moment on that roof, a tangible sensation of transcendence. God was in our midst.

As Dawn finished, all I heard on the roof was the patient's raspy, labored breath. But I am certain that an, "Amen!" thundered through God's heart. In the valley of the shadow of death, in someone's darkest hour, she fought with a quiet litany of simple prayer.

A few weeks prior to this rooftop episode, I had a patient who was really sick. A simple pneumonia kept getting more and more complicated. Test after test was ordered to figure out what pathological processes were keeping her body from healing. Through all the comings and goings that followed in those few days she was with us, she kept a death grip on a cheap, plastic, blue rosary. It was the only constant in her case. The nurses, the physicians, the aides, the medicines, the oxygen, the alarms, the needles and X-rays and procedures and diagnoses—all changed daily, even hourly. But that blue rosary never left her hand. No family or friends visited to break up her day. Apart from the staff, she was alone in that room. Her only company was that plastic symbol of hope. Her fingers locked tight around the cross dangling on the end, until it left a beaded cross imprint in her skin. She didn't understand me when I tried to explain our procedures or how the complicated disease process was destroying her body from the inside out. I tried to help her with her pain, to beat back the pneumonia, to restore her body, but nothing worked. Regardless, she wore peace like her favorite pair of old jeans, never taking it off. Exasperated after days without progress, I tried to figure out why I was more upset than she was about the lack of answers or results. I was desperate to make her better, to see an end to her suffering, but she was content.

Finally, out of ideas, I was forced to do the only thing I had not tried: to pray with her.

I had stopped praying for awhile after I became a nurse. Everything was too big, too dark and tragic. I felt like, in order to give hope to my patients, I had to offer answers like neatly wrapped Christmas presents with matching bows on top. I wanted to be the cheerful gift-giver, handing out pretty packages of quick fixes to the broken and naked. I wanted hope to be something dispensable to patients like their morning pills. If only it came in a white little cup—a few sips of water and a tip of the head, a sigh and smile as optimism spread through their arteries. But when I started working in this hospital, it felt like my hands were tied behind my back by a thousand enemies. I arrived a bouncy, bright-eyed, naïve little dreamer. That didn't last long, and neither did my prayers. I quit because they seemed to make no difference.

Half the sweaty rosary fit into my palm, while her death-grip tightened on the other. Staring at the blue beads on her white sheet, I waited for words to come. I had no plan for what to say. I suppose that I hoped heroic words of wisdom and compassion would spontaneously pour from my lips, like the apostles on Pentecost.

Running my fingers over those round smooth beads, one after another, fine chain links in between, I let the silence settle into our souls. "Father," I began haltingly. Bead followed bead followed bead followed bead. I closed my eyes and let their sequence carry me forward. "Our Father who art in heaven." Then, unbidden, my rhythm sped up as I paraphrased: "Our Dad."

Hallowed be Thy Name came next. I continued to improvise. "You are big. Totally beyond our world. I cant even begin to wrap my mind around You."

Thy kingdom come. Thy will be done. "But I am asking that You would be here. Be present here. Be real. Be all and do all that You promised You would. You say You are awesome, so we want to know it for real."

On earth as it is in heaven. "Be just as awesome and huge and crazy good right here in this hospital room as You are for all those angels up in heaven."

Give us this day our daily bread. "Because we need you just as much as we need food everyday, actually, maybe more some days." The rosary was digging as deeply into my fingers as it did in hers.

No miraculous healing took place that day. She was sick as ever, but at peace. And I realized that she wasn't clinging to the rosary because she didn't have anything else to hold on to; she clung to it because she didn't need anything else. She didn't need my answers or solutions to be at peace or to rest in hope. It wasn't about me. I was not the answer to all that she needed, but she needed me to remind her of the source of her hope—of who her hope was. Those blue beads left a mark on my heart as sure as the pattern in my palm.

Hope isn't just a plastic rosary or a prayer on a patients' deathbed. It is a way of life, a daily practice for those of us who fight to see and serve as we are called. The funny thing about hope is that it doesn't promise that everything will become perfect, as if by magic. It doesn't guarantee that suffering and pain and death will disappear forever into the distant horizon. Hope is far more visceral, sensual, tactile. It doesn't dwell in a political party or economic plan. It isn't a nice sermon or lucky lottery ticket. You won't find genuine hope in a motivational workshop or twelve step program. It doesn't come with a graduate degree or a credit rating. You can't earn it by doing acts of social justice or going on a mission trip. All those things have their place, but eventually each of them will rust and mold and fade. Death and suffering catch up with all of them.

But real hope endures, because it is confidence in and reliance on what is everlasting.

Some of us want to be hopeful but aren't. Hope can be a noun, but that's not its most powerful form. It is not most potent when it is something we have but when it is something we do. As a verb, it changes our life. Its conjugation changes lives: I hope. You hope. He, she, or it hopes. We hope. We have hoped. She is hoping. I will hope.

Hope is also a person. The Bible calls God "the hope" (Psalm 71:5: "For You God are my hope"). Hope is someone we know, a relationship we can have with a real being. It is like having a child: you get pregnant and give birth, a beautifully traumatic act. The delivery process is a fight—sometimes a deadly fight—to get that child out of you. But if you do, then you have this baby, a new little person in your life. And slowly you and that little person come to know each other. It's the same with hope. It is a battle to give birth to it, to make it a reality in your life. But if you can labor through the pain, hope enters your life as a person and builds a relationship with you.

Dawn didn't fix anything when she prayed with that family on the rooftop in the sunlight. The patient still died. She didn't cheer them up and ease their pain. They still sobbed. She didn't even give them hope as a noun. But Dawn hoped for them, she lived the verb. She fought on their behalf in the heavenly places. She brought them face-to-face, toe-to-toe with the Being who is Hope. And that is what they needed. Peace settled over them like a soft, warm summer rain. I could almost see it washing away the heaviness like streaks of dirt on a dusty car. Sorrow that was suffocating settled instead into a subtle groaning ache. Nothing disappeared, but hope appeared. Nudging gently at hearts, a presence that simply said, "You are not alone. You matter. This matters."

I get angry with the evil and abuses of this world. I can't say why it all happens, or how to stop it. I think that if I was God, I would do things differently. But I am not, and that is a good thing. Romans 8:24 tells us that, "Hope that is seen is not hope. For who hopes for what he sees?" I started to pray again when I realized that hope wasn't something I could wrap and put under the Christmas tree for my patients or a pill I could order from the pharmacy. It has nothing to do with me.

As Dawn prayed and time stood still, I watched that family standing in memoriam, standing waiting for death. I realized they didn't need me to fix them. They didn't need me to make it all go away. They needed to know Hope. And when I pray with a patient, when I do my duty and touch the naked around me, I am just a part of that birthing process. A great cloud of witnesses, including legions of nuns, rosaries in hand, stand behind me and invite me to join them in their work.

Naked. Hope.

I hate numbers. I always have.

I remember falling asleep in "class" while watching home-school algebra videos in my living room. I cried through tenth grade geometry with Mr. Marlje. To this day, I hate numbers—and the equations to manipulate them—viscerally and dramatically.

So it is ironic how much of my life revolves around them. As a nurse, I was trained to think quantitatively, to objectify and express everything with numeric precision. Like, "Mr. 704's creatinine dropped to 3.2, but his white blood cell count is 17 and hemoglobin hit 6.9. Systolic blood pressure is 70. However, his pain is only at a 5/10 and he is alert and oriented times 4. But we better do something, so let's fix him by giving 2 units packed red blood cells and holding the 40mg of furosemide, while trying a bolus of 500mL of normal saline with a dose of 500mg of Vancomycin. That should do it."

Or, "Ms. 720's SpO2 just dropped to 82%, and a quick check of her arterial blood gas lab shows a pH of 7.3 and CO2 60." Because of Ms. 720's chronic obstructive pulmonary disease, we all know she is a member of the 50/50 club, so she is only mildly retaining CO2, according to her numbers. I then watch a physician walk into her room, limply wave a stethoscope in her general direction, and lamely shrug, "You should be feeling fine. Your numbers look okay. You don't have to be afraid." He walks away, leaving her gasping and wired to the bed, her eyes bulging and rolling back in her head while she struggles for every breath. But hey, don't worry, her numbers looked okay. Twenty minutes later she's intubated in the ICU.

I could blame the system, the budget, the healthcare crisis. I could curse the Democrats or the Republicans. I do kick imaginary clumps in the tile with a vengeance, as I push through the revolving door on my way out at night after another day of banging my head against the walls of a system full of numbers that insult the dignity of my patients' right to be considered people. I may be a straight-laced, home-schooled conservative, but I could drop f-bombs all the way home. Sometimes I do.

But the system isn't the problem. It's not really about money or politics. It's me, it's all of us. All the nurses, all the patients' friends and neighbors, sometimes even their families'. We objectify the patient, because it's easier to manage what we can measure, to respond to the hard facts of existence.

It's easier to talk about numbers, about Mr. 704's statistics, than to look him in the eye and get drawn into the story of a man in the middle of crisis, who doesn't just need what can be counted and billed but needs to be seen and heard. We are all so busy responding practically that we sometimes forget that the sick and dying don't just need a quick fix or a swift end to their pain. They need to be touched. They need time, and a listening ear. They need to know that someone else remembers he or she is a human being with a story that matters. They are not just an objective problem that can be measured and solved.

Yesterday, I caught myself doing the very thing I hate when I see others do it. "Patti," I hollered, "I just checked, and your new patient in 703 has a blood sugar of 40. Want me to page someone for you?" A few minutes later I sat in 703, pushing some IV dextrose while half-listening to the patient talk about how "out of touch with reality" she felt.

Hmmm, normal with a low blood sugar, I told myself, while I tuned out what she was saying so that I could mentally run through the checklist of things that had to get done before the end of shift. I walked out of the room without once looking her in the eye or stopping to ask what she felt was going on. A few minutes later, screams erupted from room 703. Blood-curdling screams. "I am dying! Help me end it all! I am dying!" Over and over 703 cried out, while she stripped naked and thrashed around the bed. I walked in and sat next to her. Looking into her eyes (as I should have done a few minutes before), I saw panic, even terror.

"What makes you think that?" I asked.

"It's my mind. It's my mind that's sick. Sick and dying up here," she whispered, pointing a shaky finger first at her head and then at her heart.

I had a million rapid responses ready on the tip of my tongue, but I stopped. I took a moment to really look at her—for the first time—and asked, "What do you do that helps whenever you feel this way?"

She mumbled through her tears. "I pray. I pray to Jehovah. To help. But I can't. I don't have words."

The buzz outside the room—all the call lights, phones, chatter, pages, people hustling and bustling down the hallway—faded. I grabbed her hands, and asked, "Would you like me to pray for you?"

She stiffened, her naked body finally still. With now-quiet tears, she nodded. And nodded. For a good sixty seconds she nodded her head and we wept and prayed together. My tears mixed with hers on the pile of sweaty, white sheets. It wasn't an eloquent or dramatic prayer. We were both broken, and from our desperation we cried for mercy for both of us.

And for those sixty seconds, Ms. 703 was not a number.

I am so sorry, Mrs. 720, that you are a number. An accumulation of numbers on a chart, on a hospital bill. I grieve when you are no longer a person that I can see, a story that I can hear. I am sorry, Mr. 704, for making you an object to be merely measured, a problem to merely be solved. I don't want to reduce the greatest crisis of your life to an annoying task to be checked of my to do list. I don't want quantify your story. And I am sorry, Ms. 703, that it took me a while to pay attention to what you really needed, to let your heart touch mine, to make you more than a number.

Sometimes the hurt is so big, numbers are inadequate to measure it. For example, thirty is a number. So is 316,000. 1.6 million is a number. They are tangible, and they describe a fact: on January 12, 2010, a thirty-second earthquake shook Haiti. It killed 316,000 people and left 1.6 million homeless.

Like many medical professionals, I went to help. The numbers described the scale of the event, but they could not describe what it meant. When I returned, a friend asked me to reflect on the experience. Even though statistics were huge, I only had four words to describe what I experienced: hosanna (although it was desperate and gut-wrenching), truth, freedom, and hope.

These four words didn't measure what I experienced—they ran through it. They were in my hands as I stitched people back together and washed their infected wounds. They became tangible as I fixed urinals and fished for tarantulas. They comforted me as I woke in the dead of night, my plywood bunk shaking through after-shocks. They resonated as I sang in the middle of a tent-city surrounded by a people without a home. They were woven through the plots of the stories I heard of families saved and families lost. They delighted me as I learned to eat mangos like a Haitian. They kept my fears in check when I saw a government sitting in a pile of rubble. They held me up as I held a nameless, fifteen-year-old boy while he died in my arms. They were anchors in my mind when I saw devastation beyond anything I could have imagined. They reminded me that I don't know everything when I saw resilience beyond anything I expected. They cheered me up in the laughter of orphans, in the dance of children living in tent cities, in the midnight songs of communities flooded by torrential rains.

Through hundreds of thousands of words and deeds, people were crying out, "Hosanna, praise to the Lord!" They praised him for salvation, for comfort, for courage, for providing a peace that transcends understanding. Through destruction, the truth about so many things became clear to so many people. In giving what little we had, so many of us found freedom. And over and over again, I saw Jesus moving, working, speaking, singing, dancing, comforting, and healing. Time and again, I saw Jesus giving hope to people who had so little reason to hope, in a land that seemed hopeless.

Abby Jackson

As I have cared for the sick—in an inner-city hospital, in Haiti, by my grandfather's bedside—I have discovered a great paradox: hope is for the naked and hopeless.

We might assume that hope is for the healthy and the well-clothed. After all, people like that have good reasons to be hopeful. But what they call hope is really just confidence in their circumstances. They are calculating the numbers and concluding that the odds are good that they will survive in comfort. They are not necessarily sure of what they hope for, nor certain of what they do not see (as the Bible defines hope). But they are only playing odds, placing their bets on what they can see and measure.

Real hope isn't found in numbers. It can't be measured, and it isn't a function of resources or resiliency. In fact, it's only when the numbers are bad, the odds are long, and the smart bet is against our comfortable survival that genuine hope comes into play. Authentic hope is found in someone who is beyond our calculations, someone who cannot be counted or weighed or invoiced.

Hope is for the naked and hopeless. It is not for the healthy and the well-clothed. Hope comes to the sick, to those stripped of power and control. We all need God, but some of us think that He needs us. Some of us really believe in the image that we clothe ourselves in. Some of us convince ourselves that God needs that version of us. But the naked and dying know they need the Great Physician.

There is a story about Jesus that has always moved and motivated me, because it demonstrates naked hope. In Mark, chapter five, we read that:

A large crowd followed and pressed around him. And a woman was there who had been subject to bleeding for twelve years. She had suffered a great deal under the care of many doctors and had spent all she had, yet instead of getting better she grew worse. When she heard about Jesus, she came up behind him in the crowd and touched his cloak, because she thought, "If I just touch his clothes, I will be healed." Immediately her bleeding stopped and she felt in her body that she was freed from her suffering. At once Jesus realized that power had gone out from him. He turned around in the crowd and asked, "Who touched my clothes?"

"You see the people crowding against you," his disciples answered, "and yet you can ask, 'Who touched me?'"

But Jesus kept looking around to see who had done it. Then the woman, knowing what had happened to her, came and fell at his feet and, trembling with fear, told him the whole truth. He said to her, "Daughter, your faith has healed you. Go in peace and be freed from your suffering."

This woman had been suffering from menstrual bleeding for twelve years. In our culture that would be debilitating and potentially embarrassing. In her culture, it was isolating. Under the laws of the Old Testament, a woman in this condition was ceremonially unclean. As long as she was bleeding, she had to live alone. She couldn't share meals, or even cookware or cups. Most importantly, others were forbidden from touching her, lest she render someone else unclean. For twelve years, no one had touched her. She had spent every dime she had on doctors, but none could heal her, and now she was broke (something that too many of my patients experience). She was lonely, poor, and sick, stripped of all dignity and power.

And then she heard about Jesus. This rabbi was traveling the country, healing the sick and feeding the poor. And in her desperation, she joins the crowd following him. As he moves through the densely packed masses, he passes close enough for her to reach out and touch his clothes going by. In her poverty and illness, she has hope that he can heal her. But it was a tremendous risk, because in touching him, even his garments, she is contaminating this rabbi, making this prophet unclean.

He stops, and asks who touched him. His disciples don't understand the question. In this jostling crowd, hundreds of people are bumping into him. But he senses that hope, real hope, has called forth his healing power. Realizing that she cannot hide from this man, that he can see the naked truth about her, she falls trembling at his feet. She cries out for mercy . In the presence of all the people, she declares her nakedness. She is exposed, made naked, but in that nakedness, she feels for the first time like she is worth being seen and known.

And her faith heals her. Without power or prestige or anything else that most of us rely on to muscle our way through life, she is sure of what she hopes for, certain of what she cannot not see. It is in her exposure, in her nakedness that she experiences healing.

Naked we come into this world, and naked we leave. Every working day, I see naked people. But because I do, I also see hope. And I am learning to live nakedly, learning to not wrap myself in and rely on things that don't last. I want to let my vulnerability be a way for me to offer hope. I long for my soul to be healed, just as much as I long for my patients to be healed, even when my body eventually fails. Now Grandma's porcelain nurse sits on my bookshelf; a daily reminder of my own fragility and nakedness, and everyday as I pass her, I am reminded of where I find my hope.

About the Author

Abby Jackson, the author of *Naked Hope*, was born and raised in Grand Rapids, Michigan. After spending four years studying nursing at Indiana Wesleyan University, she moved back to Grand Rapids to begin her career. She is married to Tyler, a film-maker and producer. He uses cinematic story-telling for corporate advertising, non-profit documenting, and beyond.

Abby is currently enrolled at Loyola University Chicago pursuing her master's degree as a nurse practitioner.

The stories she writes are about life, disappointment, crisis, and resilience—stories that transcend sickness and health, hospitals and tragedy. It's the story of us. Of humanity exposed: an honest look at who we are without all the trappings that we layer on to hide our mess. Stories that inspire courage to face our brokenness and find healing. To read more about Abby and Tyler and the story behind *Naked Hope*, check out the website at www.nakedhope.com